HOLINESS

HOLINESS

John Webster

WILLIAM B. EERDMANS PUBLISHING COMPANY
GRAND RAPIDS, MICHIGAN / CAMBRIDGE, U.K.

First published 2003 in the U.K. by SCM Press
9-17 St Albans Place, London N1 0NX

This edition published 2003 in the U.S.A. by
Wm. B. Eerdmans Publishing Co.
2140 Oak Industrial Drive N.E., Grand Rapids, Michigan 49505 /
P.O. Box 163, Cambridge CB3 9PU U.K.
www.eerdmans.com

Printed in the United States of America

28 27 26 25 24 23   25 24 23 22 21

Library of Congress Cataloging-in-Publication Data

Webster, J. B. (John Bainbridge), 1955-
Holiness / John Webster.
p.   cm.
Includes bibliographical references and index.
ISBN 978-0-8028-2215-4 (pbk.: alk. paper)
1. Holiness — Christianity. I. Title.
BT767.W43   2003
234′.8 — dc21

2003054326

Contents

Preface

I first began to ponder the theological concept of holiness in the course of trying to construct a satisfactory account of what it might mean to speak of Scripture as 'holy'. The occasion to range more widely in the area came with the invitation to deliver the Day–Higginbotham lectures at Southwestern Baptist Theological Seminary in Fort Worth, Texas, in February 2002. The chapters of this little book are a slight amplification of the texts of those lectures as they were delivered. I am very grateful to the President and faculty of Southwestern for their invitation and their generous welcome, and to the pastors, students and theological teachers who attended the lectures and discussed them with me. I also owe a debt of gratitude to Victor Thasiah for his ready assistance in putting the material into its final form.

John Webster
Oxford, June 2002

Introduction

This book is a Christian theological essay on holiness. It is not primarily concerned with matters of ascetical or pastoral theology, though it has an eye to the implications of theological talk of holiness for the practice of the Christian life. Rather, it is written from a particular standpoint, and tries both to articulate some convictions about the substance of the Christian faith, and to set out some judgements about the nature, setting and tasks of Christian theology. At heart, what is offered here is a small exercise in dogmatic theology, a *trinitarian dogmatics of holiness*. Both parts of that designation – 'dogmatics' and 'trinitarian' – require a little more scrutiny as we approach the task which lies ahead of us.

First, what follows is a piece of Christian *dogmatic* theology. Theology is an office in the Church of Jesus Christ. It is properly undertaken in the sphere of the Church, that is, in the region of human fellowship which is brought into being and sustained by the saving activity and presence of God. Theology is one of the effects of that saving presence; it is one of the activities of reason transfigured by the renewal of human life and history which the holy God effects in his works and makes manifest in his word. The divine works of renewal culminate in the resurrection of Jesus Christ from the dead, his exaltation over all things, and his bestowal of new life in the Spirit's power. Through the Spirit, Jesus Christ the exalted one generates a new mode of common

human life, the life of the Church. To participate in that
common human life, hearing the gospel in fellowship under the
word of God and living together under the signs of baptism and
the Lord's supper, is to exist in a sphere in which God's limitless
power is unleashed and extends into the entirety of human life:
moral, political, cultural, affective, intellectual. Reason, like
everything else, is remade in the sphere of the Church; and
theological reason is an activity of the regenerate mind turned
towards the gospel of Jesus Christ, which constitutes the
Church's origin and vocation.

Theology is an office in the Church. When Church and theology are shaped into holiness by the gospel, then the work of
theology is one to which the theologian is called and appointed
and for which the theologian is equipped, in order to undertake
a particular task. Theology is not free thought or speech, if by
'free' we mean unattached to any given set of objects or any
given sphere of inquiry. Theology is not free speech but holy
speech. It is set apart for and bound to its object – that is, the
gospel – and to the fellowship of the saints in which the gospel is
heard as divine judgement and consolation – that is, the Church.
Only as it does its work under the tutelage, authority and protection of the Church is theology free. 'Church', of course, is to
be understood spiritually and not merely naturally, as the
domain in which common human life is sanctified by the Holy
Spirit and made into the communion of the saints. Theology is
under the Church's tutelage because it can only fulfil its office if
it is instructed by immersing itself in the intellectual and spiritual practices of the *sanctorum communio* in all their variety.
Theology is under the Church's authority because it is a 'positive' science, a mode of reasoned inquiry which has been given a
definite matter, apprehended in the Church of Jesus Christ in
which he makes himself known. The self-giving presence of
Christ in the Church is the law of theology, the reality which

governs theological reason. Theology is thus under the authority of the Church because the Church in its turn is under the wholly legitimate and quickening authority of the truth of the gospel. And theology is under the Church's protection because what safeguards theology's truthfulness is not the exercise of critical scruple but the fear of the one who is the Church's Lord.

What is the task of theology so described? When it is not overtaken by arbitrariness or self-confidence or scepticism about its object, theology takes its part in the work of edifying the Church. It does not do this by its own unaided powers, but by bearing witness to the risen Christ who speaks his word. Through the Spirit Christ announces his life-giving presence, nourishes the Church and makes it grow up into himself. The particular task of theology is to attest the truth of the gospel in the wake of Christ's own self-attestation. Theology edifies by testifying to the gospel as promise and claim. In the Church's theological work, the gospel is articulated as the norm of the Church's praise, confession and action, and the ground of the Church's understanding of nature and human history. As it seeks to articulate the gospel in the *sanctorum communio*, theology concentrates on two fundamental tasks, namely exegesis and dogmatics. Exegesis is of supremely critical importance, because the chief instrument through which Christ publishes the gospel is Holy Scripture. Exegesis is the attempt to hear what the Spirit says to the Churches; without it, theology cannot even begin to discharge its office. Dogmatics is complementary but strictly subordinate to the exegetical task. It is not an improvement upon Holy Scripture, replacing the informal, occasional language of Scripture by conceptual forms which are better organized, more sophisticated or more firmly grounded. Rather, dogmatics seeks simply to produce a set of flexible accounts of the essential content of the gospel as it is found in Holy Scripture, with the aim of informing, guiding and correcting the Church's reading. Dogmatics attempts a 'reading' of the gospel which in its turn assists the Church's reading. Developing such a 'reading' of the gospel entails, of course, the development (or annexation) of conceptual vocabularies and forms of argument whose range and sophistication may seem distant from the more immediate, urgent idioms of Scripture. But though technical sophistication is not without its attendant perils, it is only vicious when allowed to drift free from the proper end of theology, which is the saints' edification. When that end is kept in view and allowed to govern the work of theology, then dogmatics can be pursued as a modest work of holy reason, transparent to the gospel and doing its service in the Church as the school of Christ.

The account of holiness which is offered here is a worked example of this understanding of the task of Christian theology in its ecclesial setting. Such an understanding of theology enjoys rather little contemporary prestige, and is commonly judged to be naive, assertive, authoritarian, above all, closed. A good deal of contemporary systematic or dogmatic theology tends, by contrast, to be conversational or comparativist in approach. 'Conversational' theologies (an earlier generation might have called them 'correlational') construct Christian theology by drawing on a wide range of cultural, philosophical and religious sources to build up an account of the Christian faith through elaborating the associations and interrogations which occur as Christianity talks to others. 'Comparativist' theologies seek to identify common themes in the religions of the world and interpret them as manifestations of a single source of ultimate value. Both believe that only by resisting the confessional and the positive can Christian theology secure opportunities to make a contribution to the public realm.

By contrast, the kind of theology attempted here is less sanguine about the prospects for such exchanges. It more naturally thinks of its host culture, not as Athens, but as Babylon. It is acutely conscious of the menace of wickedness in the life of the mind. And it is intensive before it is extensive. That is, its work is focused upon a quite restricted range of texts (the biblical canon) as they have been read and struggled with in the complex though unified reality which we call the tradition of the Church. Yet although it is intensive in this way, it is not stable or settled. The persistence with which it returns to its singular theme is an attempt to face the reality of the gospel as a permanent source of unsettlement, discomfiture and renewal of vocation. The intensity of this kind of theology is not the internally-directed energy of an achieved, separated world of ideas, but that of a way of thinking which might be called eschatological – always, that is, emerging from its own dissolution and reconstitution by the presence of the holy God.

What, second, is involved in a *trinitarian* dogmatics of holiness? Put at its simplest, a trinitarian account of holiness makes two related claims. The first concerns the doctrine of God proper, namely that God is holy as Father, Son and Spirit. Second, the triune God is the Holy One *in our midst*; his holiness is a mode of relation to the creatures whom he sanctifies and calls to holiness. A dogmatic account of holiness is thus not simply concerned to offer an account of immanent divine properties; nor is it an elaboration of a spirituality or ethics of human sanctification. Rather, its concern is with the path taken by the holy three-in-one who, in the majestic fulfilment of his own freedom, elects, reconciles and perfects the creature for holy obedience. Accordingly, it does not think of divine holiness in abstraction from the sanctifying acts of God *pro nobis*, nor of human sanctity in isolation from election, salvation and the work of the sanctifying Spirit. This is the difference which the Christian doctrine of the Trinity makes in a theological account of holiness.

Although the chapters which follow are all shaped by trinitarian affirmations, there is much that they do not attempt to do. They presume, rather than defend, the view that the Christian doctrine of God is the doctrine of the Trinity; and they do not offer any treatment of the primary concepts of trinitarian theology, such as person, unity, procession, mission, and the like. Nor do they give any extended account of general questions of what is involved in predicating of God a property such as holiness. Though the book has implications for such questions, my concern here is a good deal more restricted; I try to show how a trinitarian account of God's holiness contains within it a particular way of thinking of God's relation to and action upon creatures, one which refuses both their radical separation and their confusion. Barth (somewhat bizarrely considered by many to be a reluctant trinitarian) puts the matter thus:

> Trinitarian thinking compels theology . . . to be completely in earnest about the thought of God in at least two places: first, at the point where it is a question of God's action in regard to man, and, secondly, at the point where it is a question of man's action in regard to God. It is aware of God as the Word of the Father which is spoken to man and as the Spirit of the Father and of the Word which enables man to hear the Word. It cannot seek to have merely one centre, one subject, just because its subject is God. To the extent that it sought to resolve itself into a mere teaching of God's action in regard to man, into a pure teaching of the Word, it would become metaphysics. And to the extent that it sought to resolve itself into a teaching of man's action in regard to God, into a pure teaching of the Spirit, it would become mysticism. The one, however, would be just as little a pure teaching of the Word of God, as the other would be a pure teaching of the Spirit of God. A pure teaching of the Word will take into account the

Holy Spirit as the divine reality in which the Word is heard, just as a pure teaching of the Spirit of the Son will take into account the Word of God as the divine reality in which the Word is given to us. It was with this thought in mind that the Reformers propagated the teaching of the Word of God in its correlation with faith as the work of the Holy Sprit in man.[1]

A Christian dogmatics of holiness is not metaphysics, because the holy God, reaching out into the world in Son and Spirit, is the sanctifier; nor is it mysticism (or moralism), because human reality is holy only in dependence upon the Spirit of the Son who makes holy. Thus, as Barth puts it, a trinitarian dogmatics of holiness 'cannot seek to have merely one centre, one subject' *precisely because* 'its subject is God' – God known as holy in the incarnate Word and the life-giving Spirit. And so the account of the holiness of the triune God as fellowship-creating holiness in Chapter 2 is followed in Chapter 3 by an account of the holiness of the Church and in Chapter 4 by a sketch of the individual Christian's sanctification: only in such a way can we trace to its end the trajectory of the work of the triune God. As we approach that task, however, we must first pause to consider what it means to speak of the holiness of theology.

1

The Holiness of Theology

I

What follows is a set of reflections on the holiness of God from the standpoint of Christian dogmatics. Dogmatics is often caricatured as the unholy science that reduces the practices of piety to lifeless propositions. But far from it: dogmatics is that delightful activity in which the Church praises God by ordering its thinking towards the gospel of Christ. Set in the midst of the praise, repentance, witness and service of God's holy people, dogmatics – like all Christian theology – directs the Church's attention to the realities which the gospel declares and attempts responsibly to make those realities a matter of thought. The task of this short study is to try to learn how the gospel orders our thinking in the high matter of the holiness of God.

As we approach the topic, it is imperative that we keep in mind two basic requirements for thinking Christianly about God's holiness. The first is that we need to understand that theological thinking *about* holiness is itself an exercise *of* holiness. Theology is an aspect of the sanctification of reason, that is, of the process in which reason is put to death and made alive by the terrifying and merciful presence of the holy God. Without sanctification – without being caught up by God and cleansed for the service of God in the fellowship of the saints – the work of theological reason is profitless. The second requirement for thinking Christianly about the holiness of God is that we need to make sure that we are thinking about the true God, and not about some God of our own invention. Theological talk of the holiness of God stands under the same rule as all theological talk, namely, that it is truthful only to the extent that it attempts to follow the given reality of God. That given reality is God's glorious and free self-presentation as Father, Son and Spirit, the Holy One in our midst, establishing, maintaining and perfecting righteous fellowship with the holy people of God.

In line with these two basic requirements, this first chapter addresses the question of what kind of thinking we are engaged in when we think theologically about the holiness of God. Following from this, subsequent chapters consider three primary themes: the nature of God's holiness as Father, Son and Spirit; the holiness of the Church; and the holiness of the Christian. These latter chapters will thus cover holiness in connection with the doctrine of God, the doctrine of the Church, and the doctrine of Christian sanctification. That these three themes cannot be isolated from each other is a point crucial to our understanding of them, for the holiness of the triune God is a holiness which directs itself to God's creatures as fellowship-creating holiness. God the thrice Holy One is the Holy One in our midst; and so holiness is a *relational* concept, a way of confessing that we encounter the Holy One in his works as Father, Son and Spirit or not at all.

With these thoughts in mind, we move directly to the first theme, which is the holiness of theology. To give some shape to our thinking, I offer a proposition as the basis of our reflections:

A Christian theology of holiness is an exercise of holy reason; it has its context and its content in the revelatory presence of the Holy Trinity which is set forth in Holy Scripture; it is a venture undertaken in prayerful dependence upon the Holy Spirit; it is

*an exercise in the fellowship of the saints, serving the confession
of the holy people of God; it is a work in which holiness is perfected in the fear of God; and its end is the sanctifying of God's
holy name.*

What follows simply works through the proposition, in order to
unfold for us how the gospel may order our thinking.

II

A Christian theology of holiness is an exercise of holy reason.
Christian theology is an aspect of reason's sanctification; the
founding condition for theological reason is reason's separation
by God and its being taken by God into his service. Like all other
aspects of human life, reason is a field of God's sanctifying work.
Reason, too – along with conscience, the will and the affections
– must be reconciled to the holy God if it is to do its work well.
And good Christian theology can only happen if it is rooted in
the reconciliation of reason by the sanctifying presence of God.

To speak in this way is to fly in the face of some deep intellectual and spiritual conventions of modern culture. Modernity
has characteristically regarded reason as a 'natural' faculty – a
standard, unvarying and foundational feature of humankind, a
basic human capacity or skill. As a natural faculty, reason is,
crucially, not involved in the drama of God's saving work; it is
not fallen, and so requires neither to be judged nor to be reconciled nor to be sanctified. Reason simply *is*; it is humankind in
its intellectual nature. Consequently, 'natural' reason has been
regarded as 'transcendent' reason. Reason stands apart from or
above all possible convictions, all particular, historical forms of
life, observing them and judging them from a distance. Reason
does not participate in history but makes judgements about

history; it is a transcendent and sovereign intellectual legislator, and as such answerable to none but itself.

Such conceptions of reason have become so deeply embedded in modern culture and its most prestigious intellectual institutions that they are scarcely visible to us. But for the Christian confession, these conceptions are disordered. Above all, they are disordered because they extract reason and its operations from the economy of God's dealings with his creatures. To think of reason as 'natural' and 'transcendent' in this way is, by the standard of the Christian confession, corrupt, because it isolates reason from the work of God as creator, reconciler and perfecter. Once reason is thought of as 'natural' rather than as 'created' (or, to put it differently, once the category of 'the created' is collapsed into that of 'the natural'), then reason's contingency is set aside, and its sufficiency is exalted in detachment from the divine gift of truth. Or again, when reason is expounded as a natural competency, then it is no longer understood as fallen and in need of reconciliation to God. Again, when reason is considered as a human capacity for transcendence, then reason's continual dependence on the vivifying Spirit is laid to one side, for natural reason does not need to be made holy.

Christian theology, however, must beg to differ. It must beg to differ because the confession of the gospel by which theology governs its life requires it to say that humankind in its entirety, including reason, is enclosed within the history of sin and reconciliation. The history of sin and its overcoming by the grace of God concerns the remaking of humankind as a whole, not simply of what we identify restrictively as its 'spiritual' aspect. And so reason, no less than anything else, stands under the divine requirement that it be holy to the Lord its God.

Christian theology is a particular instance of reason's holiness. Here, too – as in all truthful thinking – we are to trace what happens as reason is transformed by the judging, justifying and sanctifying work of the triune God. The sanctification of reason, moreover, involves a measure of difference: reason's transformation goes hand-in-hand with nonconformity. Holy reason is eschatological reason, reason submitting to the process of the renewal of all things as sin and falsehood are set aside, idolatry is reproved, and the new creation is confessed with repentance and delight. And, if what Paul calls the renewal of the mind (Rom. 12.2) is to be visible anywhere, it has to be in Christian theology, in which holy reason is summoned to address the great matter of God and of all things in God. Thus we move to ask: What is involved in undertaking a *holy* theology? How is this singularly demanding occupation to be characterized?

III

A holy theology *has its context and its content in the revelatory presence of the Holy Trinity.* The holy God is not merely some subject-matter entertained by the all-surveying theological mind; he is the majestic one, the one whose communicative presence makes theology possible, the one who is theology's *conditio sine qua non.*

A holy theology is responsible to revelation. That is to say, Christian theology is possible only because of the self-communicative character of the holy God of the Christian confession. That revelatory, communicative presence forms the *context* in which theology undertakes its service as holy reason; and that presence also determines the *content* of Christian theology.

Revelation may be defined as the self-presentation of the holy Trinity. It is the free work of sovereign mercy, in which the holy God wills, establishes and perfects saving fellowship with himself, a fellowship in which humankind comes to know, love and fear him above all things. We may tease this apart a little. Revelation is *the self-presentation of the holy Trinity*. Revelation, that is, is a way of talking about those acts in which God makes himself present. This means that the *content* of revelation is God's own proper reality. Revelation is not to be thought of as the communication of hidden truths, as if in revelation God were lifting the veil on something other than his own self and indicating it to us. Revelation is divine *self*-presentation; its content is identical with God. To speak of revelation is simply to point to God's speaking of his own most holy name. Moreover, the *agent* of revelation is God himself; in revelation the holy God presents himself. The making real of the presence of God is not an undertaking of an agent other than God; God is not inert or inactive but eloquent, 'speaking out' of himself. As such, revelation is a *free work of sovereign mercy*. God's revelation is God's *spiritual* presence. God is the personal subject of the act of revelation, and therefore revelation can in no way be com-modified. As spiritual presence, the presence of the holy God is free: it is not called forth by any reality other than himself, but is majestically spontaneous and uncaused.

As the holy God's self-presentation in free mercy, revelation is the establishment of *saving fellowship*. Revelation is purpo-sive. Its end is not simply divine self-display, but the over-coming of human opposition, alienation and pride, and their replacement by knowledge, love and fear of God. In short: revelation is reconciliation. Barth writes:

> This is what revelation means, this is its content and dynamic: Reconciliation has been made and accomplished. Reconcilia-tion is not a truth which revelation makes known to us; reconciliation is the truth of God Himself who grants Himself freely to us in His revelation.[1]

As the gracious presence of God, revelation is itself the establishment of fellowship. It is not so much an action in which God informs us of other acts of his through which we are reconciled to him; rather, talk about revelation is a way of indicating the communicative force of God's saving, fellowship-creating presence. God is present as saviour, and so communicatively present. This means, on the one hand, that fellowship with God is communicative fellowship in which God is known. And, on the other hand, it means that knowledge of God in his revelation is no mere cognitive affair: it is to know *God* and therefore to love and fear the God who appoints us to fellowship with himself. Revelation is thus not simply the bridging of a noetic divide (though it includes that), but is reconciliation, salvation and therefore fellowship. The idiom of revelation is as much moral and relational as it is cognitional. Revelation is the self-giving presence of the holy God which overthrows opposition to God, and, in reconciling, brings us into the light of the knowledge of God.

Such is a brief sketch of what is meant by revelation. What does it mean to say that divine revelation, so understood, is the determinative *context* of Christian theology as an exercise of holy reason? Most basically, it means that Christian theology is enclosed by, and does its work within, the sphere of the revelatory presence of the holy God. Christian theology is not a moment of intellectual detachment, a point at which the theologian steps aside from the presence of revelation and the practice of faith and adopts a different – more abstract or critical – stance towards the Christian confession. The theologian does not withdraw from the field of revelation, repentance and discipleship; indeed, he or she cannot, because there is nowhere to which the theologian can withdraw. No less than any other sphere of Christian practice, Christian theology is governed by the commanding, revelatory summons of God's presence. It takes place within the sphere marked out by that presence; and, if it withdraws from that presence or falls into an attitude of anything less than fear of the holy God, then it has simply stumbled into absurdity.

Once again, therefore, we find ourselves running up against the contradictory character of theology as an exercise of holy reason. One of the grand myths of modernity has been that the operations of reason are a sphere from which God's presence can be banished, where the mind is, as it were, safe from divine intrusion. To that myth, Christian theology is a standing rebuke. As holy reason at work, Christian theology can never escape from the sober realization that we talk in the terrifying presence of the God from whom we cannot flee (Ps. 139.7). In Christian theology, the matter of our discourse is not someone absent, someone whom we have managed to exclude from our own intellectual self-presence and about whom we can talk away safely and undisturbed. We speak in God's presence. ✱ When we begin to talk theologically about the holiness of God, we soon enough discover that the tables have been reversed; it is no longer we who summon God before our minds to make him a matter for clever discourse, but the opposite: the holy God shows himself and summons us before him to give account of our thinking. That summons – and not any constellation of cultural, intellectual or political conditions – is the determinative context of holy reason. There are other contexts, of course, other determinations and constraints in the intellectual work of theology: theology is human work in human history. But those determinations and constraints are all subordinate to, and relativized by, the governing claim of the holy God, a claim which is of all things most fearful but also of all things most full of promise.

The revelatory presence of the Holy Trinity also forms the *content* of a Christian theology of holiness. For, as the exercise of holy reason, theology does not invent its content, for its content is given to it, definitively and authoritatively, by the revelatory presence of the Holy Trinity, which is the substance of the Christian confession.

Like all Christian theology, a theology of holiness is a positive science. That is, it works both from and towards a *positum*, a given. That given we have already characterized as the communicative presence of God, Father, Son and Spirit. The astonishing reality of revelation is the content of theology as holy reason. Yet, as we shall come to see in a moment, to talk of this as the 'content' of theology may easily mislead us into thinking that theology's subject-matter is merely one more set of ideas that reason might summon before itself in an act of manipulation. Theology's content, its *object*, is always *subject*: the free, personal, utterly compelling claim of the holy God. And so theology's relation to its content is very far from that of master or inspector; much more does theology approach its given content as suppliant, penitent and disciple, for those stances most properly reflect the truth of theology's condition – its bondage to the given truth of the gospel in which alone reason may find its liberty.

Because it is bound to its object – to God as holy, self-revealing subject – theological reason does not produce its content from its own resources. Holy reason is not a *poetic* but a *receptive* enterprise; indeed, in Christian theology poetics is tantamount to idolatry. And so, when theology speaks properly of the holiness of God, its speech is not a *shaping* or *figuring* of the divine reality by the names which it gives to that reality. Its work is not what has been called 'discursive imaging activity', the generation of symbols and ciphers for God, to give some definition to an experience of the numinous.[2] If it undertakes its task in an orderly, responsible and fitting way, then theology is nothing other than an attempt to repeat the name which God gives to himself as he manifests himself with sovereign mercy: 'I am the Lord, your Holy One' (Isa. 43.15). Theology is not in the business of *naming* God, still less of fashioning whatever symbols for the divine reality may be found enriching, supportive or culturally convenient by the amateurs of religion or its despisers. In speaking of an attribute like holiness, holy reason is radically antinominalist. This is not, of course, to deny that theology has to construct language and concepts; nor is it to deny that, in undertaking that work of construction, theology does not have its own stock of ready-made words and ideas but has to borrow them from elsewhere and adapt them as best it can. To deny this would be to assume total and immediate access to God untouched by reason as human work. But in theology the work of human reason is sanctified work. Theology is reason appointed to the service of revelation, and as such its first task is to remember that in talking of God's nature it must cease to be *ratio ratiocinans* (speculative reason), and learn – painfully, contritely – to be *ratio ratiocinata*: reason which receives its matter from the self-giving of God.

IV

To sum up so far: God is not summoned into the presence of reason; reason is summoned before the presence of God. That presence, in all its infinite freedom and grandeur and grace, constitutes both the sphere in which holy reason operates, and the matter to which it must ceaselessly direct itself. How is that presence encountered? To this question, our proposition returns a simple answer: the revelatory presence of God is *set forth in Holy Scripture*. God's communicative presence is encountered through Scripture as the Holy One speaks his Word, for Holy Scripture is that creaturely instrument inspired and appointed by God to serve God's self-presentation. These texts are, to put the matter scripturally, 'from God', for in them those 'moved by the Holy Spirit spoke' (2 Pet. 1.21). Holy Scripture is the result of a divine movement; it is generated not simply by human spontaneity but by the moving power of the Holy Spirit. That moving power so orders these human, textual acts of communication that they may fittingly serve the publication of the knowledge of God. For our present purposes, this means that holy reason is exegetical reason, reason directed by and directed towards the reading of these texts which are the servants or auxiliaries of God's own speaking of his word. In the matter of God's holiness, as in all matters, the fundamental theological responsibility is exegesis.

At this point a theology of holiness finds itself at a crossroads. Here it will have to make some decisions if it is properly to demonstrate its character as the exercise of holy reason. It can go about its work in one of two ways. It can proceed by first of all elaborating a phenomenology of 'the holy', which will then form the basis of a theological account of God's holiness and its entailments for human sanctification. Or it can proceed directly to the exegetical and dogmatic tasks, bypassing the attempt to root its considerations in a religious phenomenology. I am unconvinced of the fruitfulness of the first option. That option has had and continues to have a powerful presence, both in some dominant styles of religious and cultural studies, and in those modern Christian theologies which do their work under the spell of Tillich's correlation of 'the holy' and 'the divine'. Yet in the end such phenomenologies have contributed little to constructive Christian dogmatics. Most of all, this is because in them the generic notion of 'the holy' has been accorded priority over exegesis, and has in effect swamped the specificity of a Christian understanding of holiness. For a 'positive' Christian theology, one which is strictly governed by attention to revelation through exegesis of the canon, the holiness of which the prophets and apostles speak is not a particular version of a universal religious phenomenon. The holiness of which they speak is made known in the history of God's works of creation and reconciliation; in those works God, as it were, expounds his being to us. Those works determine the content of holiness; the holiness of God and of those realities which God sanctifies is not simply 'the sacred'; it is, rather, inseparably bound to the enacted identity of this God. To say 'holy' in its Christian sense is to point to this one, to who he is and to what he does as maker, reconciler and sanctifier of his creatures. Holiness is not simply Otto's famous *mysterium tremendum*[3] or 'the quality of that which concerns man ultimately',[4] or Derrida's 'unscathed which is safe and sound'.[5] For a holy theology, abstractions like 'the holy' are best avoided, for what there is is the Holy One, the One known by the holy name, the One who has bared his holy arm. And for the knowledge of this One, what is required is exegesis of Holy Scripture.

There are two consequences here for the working of holy reason. First, because Holy Scripture is the *authoritative canon*, holy reason finds there its *norm*. To say that Holy Scripture is the authoritative canon is to say that this determinate collection of writings, received and read as a unified God-given prophetic and apostolic testimony, legitimately claims the acknowledgement, assent and obedience of the Church and its theology. The authority of Scripture for holy reason is Scripture's Spirit-bestowed capacity to quicken theology to truthful thought and speech. Truthful thought and speech follow the given order of reality. That which has authority, be it text or person, directs reason to that given order, and so forms reason's acts; authority is potent because it bears the truth to us and orders reason in accordance with reality. Hence the authority of Scripture is a matter for the Church's *acknowledgement*, not its *ascription*.

Authority cannot be conferred on Scripture by the Church or by its theology, but only greeted as that which legitimately commands the activity of reason. As such, Scripture's authority is not at all abstract or merely formal; it is the servant of the living voice of God as truth that enables the Church to live from and in the truth.

How does this norm operate? If it acts in accordance with this given norm, the work of theology must demonstrate what can be described in the most general terms as a biblical character. That is to say, it must be characterized above all by a deference to the reality of the gospel that is announced in Holy Scripture. That deference is expressed in many ways: by refusal of speculation; by resistance to the pressure to soften the imperative force of *sola scriptura* or *tota scriptura*; by the transparency of the language and concepts of theology to the scriptural canon; and above all, by the persistence, joy and humility with which holy reason addresses itself to the task of *reading* Scripture, not as master but as pupil, and by a willingness to learn in its school. All this is involved in speaking of Holy Scripture as the norm of holy reason.

Second, because Holy Scripture is *sufficient*, holy reason finds there its *limit*. The sufficiency of Scripture is an essential corollary of its authority as the inspired servant of the Word of God (indeed, it might be said that where a clear sense of the sufficiency of Scripture is lacking, one may legitimately doubt whether proper assent has been given to Scripture's authority). The sufficiency of Scripture means that in Holy Scripture may be found all that is needed for faith to know the gospel. Scripture is sufficient for its end, which is the publication of the saving knowledge of God. Holy reason therefore finds in Scripture its limit – that is, the point beyond which holy reason *may* not pass because it *need* not pass. If Scripture as *norm* requires theology to read with deference, Scripture as *limit* requires theology to demonstrate a distinctive focus in its work. That is, talk of the sufficiency of Scripture is a warning against allowing theology's imagination to be enticed into giving attention to all manner of sources of fascination; for however enriching and fruitful they may present themselves to be, in the end they nearly always constitute a distraction. Theology cannot be and do and say everything; when theology does strive to relate itself to all kinds of other fields of intellectual and cultural activity, then – however much it may do so in good faith and with praiseworthy intentions – it risks losing its determinacy, integrity and stability as the attempt to hear and repeat the one Word of God. Holy reason will therefore be characterized by a focused intensity; by getting on with its job, politely ignoring the dissuaders, declining pressing invitations to involve itself in all sorts of extramural work, and instead giving itself single-mindedly to building the walls of the city of God.

Once again, to sum up: we have been pondering the statement that, as an exercise of holy reason, a Christian theology of holiness has both its context and its content in the revelatory presence of the Holy Trinity as set forth in Holy Scripture, and that Holy Scripture thus functions as both norm and limit. From here we move to depict a little more closely how holy reason undertakes the office to which it is has been appointed. Four things are here to be noted: the *primary act* of holy reason is prayer for the assistance of the Holy Spirit; the *setting* of holy reason is the fellowship of the saints; the *manner* of holy reason is fear of the holy God; and the *end* of holy reason is the sanctifying of God's holy name. We look at each of these in turn.

V

As the exercise of holy reason, Christian theology is a *venture undertaken in prayerful dependence upon the Holy Spirit.* Holy reason, we have seen, is a human act undertaken in God's revelatory and reconciling presence. Reason does not stand apart from that presence, enjoying independence from God. Quite the contrary: if reason is to fulfil its office and to struggle towards truthful judgements, then it must be reconciled to God. This work of reconciliation is, however, the work of God himself and of God alone. It can only be God's work, for reason's alienation from truth entails reason's incapacity. Alienated from the given order of God's truth and repudiating its calling as God's creature, reason subverts that relation to the holy God which is the essential condition for knowledge of the truth. In Paul's terms in Rom. 1: reason is absolutely jeopardized by the creature's refusal to glorify God or exist in gratitude, and so reason becomes futile, senseless and dark. Out of that futility, senselessness and darkness is born idolatry, that fateful exchange of truth for lies, and of worthy objects of worship and service for images. Calvin comments:

> [T]hey forsook the truth of God and turned aside to the vanity of their own reason, which is completely undiscriminating and impermanent. Their *senseless heart* being thus darkened could understand nothing correctly, but in every way was borne headlong into error and falsehood. This was their unrighteousness, that the seed of true knowledge was immediately choked by their wickedness before it grew to maturity.[6]

Of such vanity, God alone can cure us. This God does through the work of the Holy Spirit. The Spirit judges, slays and regenerates reason to the end that it may once again fulfil its calling, honouring and giving thanks to God. Through the Holy Spirit, God's holiness is brought to bear on the work of reason. As we shall come to see in the next chapter when we turn to look more directly at holiness as a divine attribute, God's holiness may be understood under two aspects. One is what the great theologian of the attributes of God Hermann Cremer called 'God's active opposition to sin' (*die Gegenwirkung Gottes gegen die Sünde*); the other is God's sanctification or separation of creaturely instruments for the service of his glory.[7] God's holiness as *opposition* is undertaken in the Spirit's work of *mortificatio* (putting to death); God's holiness as *sanctification* is undertaken in the Spirit's work of *vivificatio* (making alive). And both can – indeed must – be extended into a Christian description of the work of reason, and so of theology. Such a description does not, of course, entail a denial of the creatureliness of our intellectual activity (any more than to talk of human moral sanctity is to undermine our sense that we are, indeed, moral agents). What it does is specify what *kind* of creaturely activity we are engaged in when we do the works of holy reason. The kind of creaturely activity we are engaged in is, I suggest, best described as a dying and rising again.

Holy reason is mortified reason. It is reason which has been judged and destroyed as it has been set under the judgement of God against what Paul calls 'all ungodliness and wickedness of men who by their wickedness suppress the truth' (Rom. 1.18). That judgement and destruction was effected once for all at the cross of the Son of God, the one in whose dying God destroyed the wisdom of the wise (Isa. 29.14; 1 Cor. 1.18–19). And holy reason continues to live out mortification as it carries the dying of Jesus within itself – that is, as it submits to the requirement of unceasing repentance, as the Spirit of holiness reproves reason's idolatry, pride, vain curiosity and ambition, as – in short –

reason unlearns falsehood and is taught the truth. Holy reason is also reason made alive. If it is subject to the Holy Spirit's reproof as Lord, it is no less subject to the same Spirit's regenerative work as the giver of life. Through the life-giving Spirit, reason is given direction, and thereby turned to its proper end, which is the knowledge of the holy God and of all things in him. And through the Spirit, reason is made capable: its calling renewed, reason is instructed and equipped by the Spirit. And, through this sanctifying work of the Spirit, reason becomes 'holy', set apart by God so that it may undertake the ministry for which it was both made and remade.

This is why the venture of theological reason can only be undertaken in prayer for the coming of the Holy Spirit. Because theological work is always a process of mortification and regeneration, at its heart is the act of beseeching God for instruction:

> Make me to know thy ways, O Lord;
> teach me thy paths.
> Lead me in thy truth, and teach me . . . (Ps. 25.4–5)

Such prayer is not merely ornamental in theology; it is of the essence. In prayer reason looks to God, confessing its inadequacy and its need to be led into God's truth, and trusting confidently in the Spirit's instruction:

> The first and basic act of theological work is *prayer* . . . [T]heological work does not merely begin with prayer and is not merely accompanied by it; in its totality it is peculiar and characteristic of theology that it can be performed only in the act of prayer.[8]

To speak thus of intellectual work may sound strange, even ludicrous: can such an account be anything other than a hopelessly idealized, even mythological, account of the rational activities which make up the study of divinity? And faced with this suspicion, might it not be less embarrassing to make a much softer claim – about the pious disposition or spiritual virtues of the theologian? But talk of theology as the exercise of holy reason is not just talk of a certain setting of the theologian's affections; in the last analysis, holiness is not a psychological or a religious quantity. Reason is holy because God acts upon reason, arresting its plunge into error and freeing it from its bondage to our corrupt wills and our hostility to God. And to describe theological work as a work of holy reason is to say that, without talk of this God and his acts of judgement and renewal, we cannot depict what happens when we take it upon ourselves to venture the work of the theologian.

VI

Next, as holy reason theology is *an exercise in the fellowship of the saints, serving the confession of the holy people of God.* God's holiness, we shall come to see, is fellowship-creating holiness. The holiness of God is confessed in the Christian tradition as the holiness of the triune God, the One made known as Father, Son and Spirit, the One who turns to his creation as its maker, reconciler and perfecter. It is, accordingly, a holiness which assembles and upholds a human community, set apart as the communion of saints to be the human answer to God's holy love. And theology is an undertaking of this *sanctorum communio*, reason designated to serve the community's confession of the Holy Trinity.

Because of this, first, theology is an *activity undertaken within the fellowship of the saints.* The realm of theology is the realm of the Church. Theology partakes of the same holy things as does the Church. It hears the same gracious Word of God in the gospel; it stands beneath the same judgement which that Word pronounces, and receives the same absolution from the Word; it is nourished and renewed by the same Spirit through Scripture and sacrament; it is a participant in the same praise and petition; it directs itself by the same confession; it, too, is marked by the same separation from the wickedness which profanes God's holy name. Though the institutional arrangements of theology in modernity have often made it hard for us to see this point, theology is not a *transcendent* moment, some activity of the mind standing above the merely domestic life of the Christian community and submitting it to an ironic, critical gaze. Holy reason is ecclesiastical science – a knowing and inquiring which takes place within 'the commonwealth gathered, founded, and ordered by the Word of God', and participating in the calling and promise which God issues to that commonwealth.[9] Modernity, of course, denies the title 'science' to any such activity, just as it denies the title 'reason' to those intellectual acts which take their rise in the confession of the gospel. But those denials tell us more about modernity than they do about science or reason, and a confident, holy theology will not be too troubled by them, but simply fulfil its office with diligence and with deference to the call of God in the fellowship of the saints.

Theology is, second, an exercise of *fellowship with the saints.* As it does its work in the commonwealth of God's people, theology renders its assistance to the community to which it belongs. Its particular ministry is to help in the edification of the Church, building up the Church's common life and so serving the confession of the gospel. Theology does this, very simply, by giving an account of the substance of the gospel as that to which all speech, thought and action in the Church must conform. In the work of holy reason, the communion of saints submits its life to the gospel's appraisal, testing its apprehensions of God by judging them against the one norm of all truth, God's revelatory presence as holy Word. As it does its theology, the Church inquires whether it really speaks, thinks and acts as the communion of saints; whether the gospel has been truly, repentantly and fully heard; whether the promises and commands of the gospel have been acknowledged in all their authority and grace; whether in their confession of the gospel the elect of God are truly holy and blameless before him. Crucially, however, theology does not perform this task as the Church's Lord or judge. How could it? The Church has only one Lord and judge, the Holy One himself, whose office theology may not arrogate to itself. Rather, theology's critical work is undertaken by exemplary submission to the gospel – by theology itself standing beneath the Word of God which assembles the community, by governing its own speech and thought by the given truth of the gospel, above all, by looking to God, acknowledging that, like all things in the life of the Church, theology is impossible unless God makes it possible. Only in this way – humbly and without pretence – can holy reason stand in fellowship with the saints of God and serve their confession.

VII

Our next clause draws together the foregoing by indicating something of the manner of theology as holy reason. Theology is a work in which *holiness is perfected in the fear of God.* The perfection of holiness – that is, its completion or fulfilment – involves the fear of God (2 Cor. 7.1). Holiness is set out by Paul in 2 Cor. 6 as a cleansing which involves both a radical separation from that which is unclean, and also fellowship with God the Father. And holiness reaches its completeness in the fear of the Lord who is the beginning of wisdom. What does this mean for theology as holy reason?

Theology exists under the same condition as all other activity in the life of faith, namely, that it is done in the presence of the Holy One who 'meets us as unconditional majesty'.[10] Because God is majestic and therefore to be feared before all things, to encounter him is to be encountered by that which we can never master, which can never become an object, an idea or pattern of words or experience that we can retrieve and inspect at will. The holy God is utterly free; even in his approach to humankind in which he elects and sanctifies a people for himself, he is not a disposable asset, an entity which can become part of the religious or cultural stock of his people. 'You shall not profane my holy name, but I will be hallowed among the people of Israel; I am the Lord who sanctify you' (Lev. 22.32). This requirement – that God be feared and his name hallowed – is in many respects *the* requirement for theological reason. Reason can only be holy if it resists its own capacity for idolatry, its natural drift towards the profaning of God's name by making common currency of the things of God. A holy theology, therefore, will be properly mistrustful of its own command of its subject-matter; modest; aware that much of what it says and thinks is dust. God's holiness means that theology stands under the prohibition: 'Do not come near' (Ex. 3.5). Accordingly, theology will be characterized less by fluency and authority, and much more by weakness, a sense of the inadequacy of its speeches to the high and holy matter to which it is called to bear testimony.

Nevertheless, this prohibition is not an absolute moment by which reason is entirely incapacitated. Alongside the prohibition stands with equal force an imperious command to speak: 'Who has made man's mouth? . . . Is it not I, the Lord? Now therefore go, and I will be with your mouth and teach you what you shall speak' (Ex. 4.11–12). The command is also a promise – that God will make holy reason capable of that of which sin makes it incapable; that because the speeches of reason are in the hands of God, they may also serve in the indication of the gospel's truth. Idolatry is reproved, not by silence, but by ✡ speeches that set forth what God has taught. And in such speeches, holy reason gives voice to the fear of God.

VIII

What, finally and very briefly, is the end or *telos* of the work of theology as holy reason? It is what Jonathan Edwards called 'an high esteem of God',[11] a *sanctifying of God's holy name*. The sanctifying or hallowing of the holy name of God is, as we shall come to see later, the basic end of all the works of the fellowship of the saints:

> Let them praise thy great and terrible name!
> Holy is he! (Ps. 99.3)

or again:

> My mouth will speak the praise of the Lord,
> and let all flesh bless his holy name for ever and ever.
>
> (Ps. 145.21)

Praise, blessing and sanctifying add nothing to God; they do not and cannot expand or enrich God's holiness, which is inexhaustibly and unassailably full and perfect. They are simply an acknowledgement and indication. And theology as holy reason finds its completion in such acknowledgement and indication.

To talk of the end of reason in these terms is once again to refuse to segregate intellectual activity from other acts of discipleship. Holy reason is a practice in the life of the communion of the saints; as such, it partakes in the movement of the Church, sharing its origin and participating in its goals. To abstract holy reason from that movement is to arrest its course. And not only that, neglect of the true ends of the intellectual activity of theology in the praise of God nearly always involves their substitution by other ends, the elevation of technical, historical or philosophical reason, and their detachment from repentant and joyful service of God's holy name. One could organize an entire history of modern theology around that theme: the intellectual afflictions which have attended the progressive detachment of reason from piety.

None of this should be taken as a suggestion that holy reason is other than a human activity. Theology is not inspired; it is not a sacrament of the gospel; it does not have the authority of the teaching office in the Church. It is not a means of grace, but the human work of thinking and speaking about the holy God. Because it is always a human work, it participates in the frailty and fallibility of its practitioners and of their times. Theology's reference to revelation does not raise it out of the stream of all other human rational endeavour. Yet *in* – not *despite* – its very human character, theology can be holy reason. It can serve the Holy One and the congregation which gathers around him, wrestling with him, beseeching his blessing, and then like Jacob limping on its way.

2

The Holiness of God

I

The first chapter reflected on one of the two basic requirements for thinking Christianly about the holiness of God, namely that because such thinking does its work in the presence of the self-giving holy God, it must be a work of holy reason, reason consecrated to the service of the holy God in the communion of his saints. Reason's task in this matter is to 'exhibit' God's 'wonderful name'.[1] That holy name, which God himself speaks and to which theology must give reason's reverence, is his name as Father, Son and Holy Spirit. Only as it is a repetition of that name can our thinking about the holiness of God himself be governed by the second basic requirement for all Christian thinking about God, namely, that it must be thinking which is concerned with the true God.

As we turn, then, to consider holiness as a divine attribute, our task is to outline a trinitarian dogmatics of the holiness of God. Dogmatics, once again, is not a speculative enterprise, a conceptual improvement upon the gospel as it is announced in Holy Scripture. The objective of dogmatics is very simple: again in Calvin's words, to provide 'godly minds with a sort of index to what they should particularly look for in Scripture concerning God'.[2] And to guide us on our way, another proposition:

*God's holiness is the holiness of Father, Son and Spirit, the one
who bears his holy name, who is holy in all his works, and who
is the Holy One in our midst, establishing, maintaining and
perfecting righteous fellowship with the holy people of God.*

II

God's holiness is the holiness of Father, Son and Spirit. All the
attributes of God are identical with God's essence; but his
essence is his being and act as Father, Son and Holy Spirit. God
is holy in his triune being and activity. Thus when, in accordance with the Christian confession, we talk of the holiness of
God, the God of whom we speak is *this* God; and what theology
is required to say about holiness is determined at every point by
the fact that it is confessed of this one.

From the very outset, this means that a trinitarian dogmatics
of holiness has to follow a quite distinctive path, one already
marked out for it by the self-presence of God, yet one to which
it can only adhere by a measure of resoluteness, as well as by a
measure of cheerful freedom from the conventions of neigh-
bouring fields of rational activity. The distinctiveness can be
brought out by noting three particular demarcations.

First, however disapproving its postmodern neighbours
may be, however sheerly atavistic it may seem, a trinitarian
dogmatics of the holiness of God will be an exercise in 'ontotheology'. For its concern is – with fear and trembling – to give
a conceptual depiction of the Church's confession of the works
and ways of the Holy Trinity. And such a depiction necessarily
requires an ontology – an account of the being, nature and
properties of God. This ontology must certainly be resolutely
dogmatic, that is, governed by the gospel's annunciation of the
history of God with us; and it must, therefore, of necessity be

engaged in a dispute with metaphysical theism about the nature of God. But dogmatics ought to be unpersuaded that Christian theology can long survive the abandonment of ontotheology, and ought to think long and hard before it hands over the doctrine of God for deconstruction. The undeniably corrosive effects of certain traditions of metaphysics are best retarded, not by repudiating ontology, but by its fully Christian articulation.

Second, the distinctiveness of a trinitarian dogmatics of the holiness of God will be shown in its lack of interest in making use of religious phenomenology as a foundation for positive Christian teaching, or in correlating its findings with inquiries into the phenomena – cultural, anthropological and religious – of 'the holy'. The remarkable prestige enjoyed by Rudolf Otto's work *Das Heilige* over much of the last century is partly explicable by the companionability of his project to a wide range of theologians – by no means simply of revisionist leanings – who found in the concept of 'the holy' a ground or correlate or parallel for some of the things which Christian theology has to say about God. Paul Tillich wrote:

> Holiness is an experienced phenomenon; it is open to phenomenological description. Therefore, it is a very important cognitive 'doorway' to understanding the nature of religion, for it is the most adequate basis we have for understanding the divine. The holy and the divine must be understood correlatively.[3]

Much might be said by way of critical reflection on the project which Tillich announces: its appeal to generics such as 'religion' and 'the divine'; its intellectualist assumption that 'understanding' the divine is superior to practice; and its foundationalist entanglements. In dogmatic terms, however, the most problematic feature is the detachment of holiness from personal divine *imply that God cannot look on sin?*

presence and action. From this perspective, Tillich's definition of holiness to which reference was made earlier – 'the *quality* of that which concerns man ultimately' – seems a curiously lame account of the matter, in which the Lutheran *pro me* is dissolved into a modulation of human selfhood, lacking reference to the force and sheer particularity of God's self-communicative presence that dogmatics must struggle to retain.

Third, a trinitarian dogmatics of God's holiness will find itself at a distance from important features of the accounts of the divine attributes offered in some dominant styles of analytical philosophical theology. The reader of such work is immediately struck by the absence of serious engagement with divine holiness in the presentations of the attributes of God that are offered there, and the distinct preference for devoting the lion's share of attention to the so-called metaphysical attributes such as omnipotence or omniscience.[4] The reasons for this neglect are varied: a strange incapacity to deal with the positivities of particular religious beliefs and practices; a corresponding preference for highly abstract, simplified renderings of the content of Christian belief as a version of 'natural religion'; a reluctance to allow trinitarian doctrine to play any fundamental role in shaping an account of God's being; the isolation of discussion of the attributes of God from consideration of the works of God in the economy of salvation. But all these features are undergirded by the way in which priority is often given to questions of the essence of God over questions of the character of God's existence.[5] One immediate effect of this prioritizing is that metaphysics as the science of being has precedence over exegesis and dogmatics (which are simply the domestic reflection of the ecclesial congregation), since metaphysics, from the early modern period, has assumed responsibility for the task of developing an account of first principles.[6] Modern analytical philosophical theology is in many respects a continuation of that division of labour, especially when the overall project of philosophical theology is conceived to be that of giving 'reasons for the rational intelligibility of the world and of human being in the world in the framework of a *conception of God*'.[7] The *use* of the concept of God in this way – its deployment in the task of complete explanation – shapes its *content*.

Two consequences are to be noted. First, when the concept of God is shaped by proofs for the existence of God which themselves serve to underwrite a complete explanation of reality, then considerable weight is attached to the so-called metaphysical attributes of God:

> The interpretation of reality which is provided by the theistic proofs is only coherent if God can be seen as a being with specific attributes. As the universal ground of existence and explanation God must be understood as necessary, immutable, uncaused, omnipotent, eternal, omnipresent, omniscient and in every respect perfect.[8]

Holiness tends to be a casualty of this process because it is apparently less crucial in laying out what kind of being God must be conceived to be if he is to be the ground of the world's existence. Second, this use of the concept of God characteristically restricts the relation between God and the creation to one between causal power and product; language of God as personal agent-in-relation scarcely features. Once again, therefore, holiness recedes from view, for as a 'relative' or 'personal' attribute holiness is less important in giving an account of God as the world's ontological ground. But, as we shall come to see, a trinitarian dogmatics, its attention focused on the being of God as displayed in God's work in the economy, will be uneasy with the distinction between metaphysical and relative attributes, and will seek assiduously to root its account of God's holiness in the specifically Christian confession of God as Father, Son and Spirit. It will seek to avoid the mistake of abstraction: the mistake, that is, of thinking that the doctrine of the Trinity makes no real difference. For the Christian confession, the doctrine of the Trinity makes all the difference in the world, for that doctrine is at the heart of the Christian gospel, and so at the heart of the Christian understanding of the nature of God and of the manner of God's relation to the world. The doctrine of the Trinity is the Christian understanding of God; and so the doctrine of the Trinity shapes and determines the entirety of how we think of God's nature, including how we think of God's holiness. In short: God is holy as Father, Son and Spirit.

III

God's holiness is the holiness of Father, Son and Spirit, that is, *the holiness of the One who bears his holy name.* Like all the attributes of God, the attribute of holiness is an indication of the name of God. God's *name* is his enacted identity, God's sheer, irreducible particularity as *this One* who is and acts *thus.* God's name is his incomparability, his uniqueness. Bearing this name, God is not simply holy mystery, the nameless and voiceless whence of some sense of the numinous, an ineffable and indefinite deity. In his unalterable and unassailable majesty he is the one who he is: the self-determining one, wholly beyond the reach of any comparison or class: 'I am the Lord, that is my name' (Isa. 42.8).[9]

As the one who is utterly incomparable, who is in every respect *a se,* God names himself. The name which God *bears* is the name which God *speaks.* When human speech takes it upon itself to repeat this name, whether in praise or proclamation or in the work of holy reason, God's name is not ascribed but confessed; God receives his name from no one but himself, for his identity is altogether self-originating. Theological talk of the divine attributes is, correspondingly, not a *proposal*, a projection of a category onto God, a naming. It is, rather, a repetition of God's name, a conceptual expansion of that name which does not add to it or go beyond it, but simply utters it as it has already been uttered, returning to it as that which cannot be enhanced, or mastered, or resolved into anything other than itself. All theological talk of the attributes of God traces God's own enactment of his name; and so theological talk of God's holiness simply says: 'the Lord, he is God; the Lord, he is God' (1 Ki. 18.39).

Theological talk of the divine attributes is thus not primarily a matter of categorization but of confession; the attributes of God are conceptual glosses on God's name, indicators of God's identity. It was for this reason that the classical dogmatic tradition insisted that when theology enumerates a range of different attributes of God, it is not denoting different realities within the divine being; rather, each of the attributes designates the totality of the being of God under some particular aspect. That is to say, language about the different divine attributes must not compromise the principle which Augustine enunciated in saying that God is 'simple beyond all comparison'.[10] God's simplicity means that God is beyond composition; different divine attributes do not, therefore, denote separate parts of God which, when assembled, together make up the divine identity. Rather, the enumeration of divine attributes is simply a designation of God's simple essence. The attributes are not *accidentia*, accidental qualities in God by virtue of which God can be said to be, for example, holy or wise, for God is *essentially* holy and wise. 'In God,' as Augustine puts it, 'to be is the same as . . . to be wise.'[11] Thus the range of the divine attributes indicates nothing other than the divine essence in its purity and simplicity.

Accordingly, classical dogmatics was reluctant to allow that the divine attributes may be distinguished *realiter* – this, because of a desire to maintain that 'every attribute is a manifestation of the same absolutely simple essentiality of God'.[12] The danger – of which classical dogmatics was sharply aware – was that such an affirmation might quickly slip into nominalism. For if a powerful doctrine of the simplicity of God leads us to assert that the various attributes of God are distinguished merely *rationaliter*, then scepticism can follow: talk of the divine properties is left unattached to the divine reality, and God can easily become a blank, unnameable void.[13] As a safeguard, it is important to maintain that, although the distinctions which reason makes between the different divine attributes do not correspond in any straightforward way to distinctions within God's most simple being, they are, for all that, not merely rational or notional distinctions. They are distinctions which are founded upon the reality of that by which reason is accosted – the self-presence of God as creator, reconciler and perfecter; and so they are the work of *ratio ratiocinata*, and not merely mental projections:

> To our so-called formal concepts, really differentiated from each other, there answer on God's side various objective concepts, the note of which in God is but the one infinite perfection, apprehensible by our understanding, owing to its native finitude and weakness, only in various acts, in parts as it were.[14]

This sounds fiercely abstract; but underlying its formality is a deep principle of all Christian talk of God, namely that such talk is an indication of the pure and singular act of God's being, his being for himself by his being for us in his merciful work as Father, Son and Spirit. God's simplicity is his irreducible 'this-ness', executed in the drama of his works. The simple act in

which God is who he is is the act of what Jüngel calls 'the *concrete
simplicity* of God'.[15] To talk of God's simplicity, and thus of
God's attributes as all denoting that simplicity, is not to reduce
God to a point (pure will, perhaps, or pure cause), but to refer to
the 'inexhaustible fullness' of God's triune being and act.[16]
God's simplicity is God's singular plenitude, what Augustine in
a lovely phrase calls 'simple multiplicity or manifold simplicity',
and what I have called God's 'name' or 'enacted identity', the
fullness from which we have all received, grace upon grace.

To sum up, therefore: when theology speaks of the attributes
of God, it is attempting a rich set of conceptual enlargements
upon God's concrete simplicity, the rendition of his identity
which God gives as the one who is. God's love, mercy, patience,
righteousness and holiness, God's infinity, impassibility,
changelessness and omnipotence, all say one thing, at once most
simple and most comprehensive: *God is*. The content of the
term 'holiness' in the case of God is wholly determined by its
reference to God's person. The predicate (holy) is exhaustively
defined by the subject (the triune God). Holiness, the Romanian
Orthodox theologian Staniloae remarks, is not 'the attribute of
impersonal mystery' but 'the attribute of transcendence as
person'.[17] That is, holiness is a predicate of the personal being,
action and relation of the triune God, of God's concrete execution of his simplicity; it is not a quality in abstraction, but an
indicator of God's 'name'.[18]

IV

As Father, Son and Spirit, God is *holy in all his works*. God *is*
holy; but God is what God does, and so *God's holiness is to be
defined out of God's works*. The determining context for talk of
God's holiness is the examination of the 'economy' of God's

works. By 'the economy', we refer to the comprehensive scope of God's dealings with creation and humanity – as creator, as saviour, and as the one who will bring his purposes to perfection. The panorama of what the triune God does is the execution of God's being. And because God's identity is enacted in his works, theological reflection upon God's attributes is to proceed on the basis of the given reality of God's making himself known as the Father, the Son and the Spirit, who stands in relation to the world and is at work in the world as its creator, saviour and perfecter. For the Christian confession, there is no other God than this one; God's essence and nature, and therefore God's holiness, are to be perceived here, in God's works, or they are not perceived at all.

Starting here has especially important consequences for an account of divine holiness. The divine attributes, I have suggested, are ways of offering a gloss on the divine name, an indication of God's identity as lordly reconciler and redeemer. One rather formal way of making this point would be to say that the attributes of God are what have been called 'character trait predicates', that is, ways of talking which 'call attention to patterns in a person's behaviour across time'.[19] Such predicates are ways of identifying the intentional action of persons; and, in the case of the divine attributes, this means that 'God will bear these personal attributes as an agent whose identity is made manifest in action'.[20] Another, rather more directly dogmatic, way would be to say that the attributes of God articulate the history of God's conduct towards us:

> As a description of the divine essence . . . every predication of God is a short-hand recounting that expresses the divine self-relation on the basis of God's conduct towards us . . . Predications of God *identify who* God is in that they *describe what* God is. Thus, they *recount who and what* God is . . .

[T]he basic attributes of the divinity of God are conceptual-
ized on the basis of the fundamental context of the history of
God.[21]

Holiness is a mode of God's activity; talk of God's holiness
identifies the manner of his relation to us. For if the word 'holy'
is a shorthand term for a pattern of activity, if it indicates – as
von Rad put it – 'a relationship more than a quality', then the
holy God is precisely God manifest to humankind in his
gracious turning.[22] 'God's holiness', wrote Bavinck, 'is revealed
in his entire revelation to his people, in election, in the
covenant, in his special revelation, in his dwelling among
them.'[23]

What, then, we may ask, is the force of faith's language of
God's holiness? What particular aspect of the unified identity
of the triune God's being, works and ways is indicated by this
language? We may answer thus: Talk of God's holiness denotes
the majesty and singular purity which the triune God is in
himself and with which he acts towards and in the lives of his
creatures, opposing that which is itself opposed to his purpose
as creator, reconciler and perfecter, and bringing that purpose
to its completion in the fellowship of the saints. Holiness,
because it is the holiness of the God and Father of our Lord Jesus
Christ now present in the Spirit's power, is pure majesty in
relation. God's holy majesty, even in its unapproachableness, is
not characterized by a sanctity which is abstract difference or
otherness, a counter-reality to the profane; it is a majesty known
in turning, enacted and manifest in the works of God. Majesty
and relation are not opposed moments in God's holiness; they
are simply different articulations of the selfsame reality. For if
God's relation to us were merely subordinate to his primary
majesty, then God's essence would remain utterly beyond us,
forever hidden; and if God's relation to us were not majestic,

then that relation would no longer be one in which we encountered God. An essential condition, therefore, for making dogmatic sense of God's holiness is to avoid the polarizing of majesty and relation; the divine distance and the divine approach are one movement in God's being and act.[24] In short: the holiness manifest in the works of the majestic triune God is manifest as *personal, moral relation,* as a relation between the persons of the Holy Trinity and the creatures whom God summons into holy fellowship with himself.[25] One immediate corollary here is that the familiar distinctions between the absolute or metaphysical and relative or personal attributes of God can have only limited application. When deployed to best advantage, those distinctions attempt to maintain that God is free in relation to the creation, and that God's freedom is precisely his freedom for relation. But the distinctions can quickly become vicious, if they are allowed to erode the coherence of God's being *ad intra* and his being *ad extra,* or to drive a wedge between the essence and the existence of God, by suggesting that there are *non-relational* (metaphysical) divine attributes. The attribute of holiness is particularly difficult to assimilate into the absolute–relative scheme, whose severe limitations it thereby exposes. For like an absolute attribute, holiness stresses the divine transcendence; and like a relative attribute, holiness also draws attention to God's work as the world's creator, reconciler and sanctifier. Holiness is thus a telling illustration of the twofold rule articulated by Martensen: '[t]here are no divine attributes, which . . . do not express a relation of God to the world'; and 'there are no divine attributes . . . which do not go back on God himself'.[26]

God *is* holy, and therefore holiness characterizes all God's ways; in all that he does he is holy, and can no more not be holy than he can not be God. As all God's ways are merciful and true; as all his ways are the exercise of his omnipotence; so all God's

ways are holy. Holiness pervades all God's works; it is what
Aulén calls 'the background and the atmosphere of the conception of God'.[27] The pervasiveness of holiness in all talk of
God has led some to suggest that holiness ought not to be
treated as a separate attribute, taking its place in a sequential
exposition of all the divine perfections, but rather should be
expounded first as what it is, an ingredient within all God's
attributes.[28] The dogmatic instinct here is a sound one, and
organizing the material in this way is not without its advantages.
Nevertheless, the instinct needs to be followed with some
caution, above all lest it lead to an assimilation of holiness to
divine aseity, once again compromising not only the relational
character of the holiness of the holy Trinity, but also the
identity of God's being *in se* with his turning to us. As Cremer
puts the matter: 'Through the revelation of God's holiness, the
real deity of God becomes truly revealed . . . [Holiness] is the ironic
decisive attribute for knowing and acknowledging God and for
understanding his will and action; on this attribute, all other
knowledge of the attributes of God depends. If the holiness of
God is not perceived and understood, then the entire work and
conduct of God are not grasped.'[29]

V

As Father, Son and Spirit, God is *the Holy One in our midst,
establishing, maintaining and perfecting righteous fellowship with
the holy people of God.*

 To sum up so far: God the Holy Trinity is known in his turning to us, and so to speak of God's holiness is to speak on the
basis of his majestic self-communicative and saving presence.
God the Holy One is the Holy One *in our midst*. The crucial consequence of this for how we think about the holiness of God is

that the idea of God's holiness is a *relational* concept. That is to say, what it articulates is the origin, manner and goal of the relation in which God stands to his creation.

In highlighting the relational character of God's triune holiness, we are not subjectivizing this attribute, translating it into a way of talking about ourselves and our way of experiencing and relating to God. To say that would be to fall into some of the snares that have entangled accounts of God's attributes in Western theology since the great early-nineteenth-century Reformed theologian Schleiermacher. 'All attributes which we ascribe to God are to be taken as denoting not something special in God, but only something special in the manner in which the feeling of absolute dependence is to be related to Him.'[30] Schleiermacher's famous definition is intended to deny what he calls the 'speculative character' of the divine attributes and to restore their soteriological import.[31] Yet this indisputably praiseworthy undertaking quickly unravels. For where Schleiermacher was cautiously referential, his heirs have often become nominalist, even sceptical. When the divine attributes become primarily ways of characterizing religious apprehensions of the divine, apprehensions filled out culturally and experientially, then God's own being is at best left indefinite, and at worst becomes a blank, a void which we then have busily to fill with ideas of our own invention. Over against this, talk of God's holiness does indeed indicate God's being. But because it indicates the being of *this* God, the triune God of the Christian confession, it speaks, not of God in abstraction from us, but of God's presence as the one who turns to us in mercy and grace. God's holiness is made known to us in the way in which, as Father, Son and Spirit, God enters into relation with us and deals with us as creator, saviour and sanctifier. This relation – this turning, this merciful movement of God in which in utter freedom the holy God does indeed direct himself towards us – is the place where God manifests himself to us, and so the place where his being is made known. The holy God is who he is in his works, and his works are his directing of himself to us as creator, saviour and sanctifier. On the basis of a consideration of these works – and only on that basis – we are to discern the holiness of God.

It is difficult to overstress the importance of this relational character for grasping the nature of God's holiness. It is fatally easy to think of God's holiness simply as a mode of God's sheer otherness and transcendence – that is, as the opposite of relational; as concerned, not with God *with* us, but with God *apart from* us. But to follow that path is radically to misunderstand the biblical testimony. The holiness of God is not to be identified simply as that which distances God from us; rather, God is holy precisely as the one who in majesty and freedom and sovereign power bends down to us in mercy. God is the Holy One. But he is the Holy One 'in your midst', as Hosea puts it (Hos. 11.9); or as Isaiah puts it: 'great in your midst is the Holy One of Israel' (Isa. 12.6).

Consequently, God's holiness is not simply to be associated with his transcendence, but equally with his condescension. Put another way: God's transcendence is not different from or other than the freedom in which the holy God condescends to move towards the world and humankind. In particular, it is important to maintain that God's holiness is inseparable from the fact that God is the covenant God. God is the Holy One *of Israel*, which means to say that God is holy precisely in calling a people to be his own people, in purifying them, and in maintaining them against all threats so that they may be his own possession. Thus the famous imperative in Leviticus – 'You shall be holy for I the Lord your God am holy' (Lev. 19.2) – does not envisage God's holiness simply as God's distance or utter difference, but rather as that which is known in God's covenant-creating activity. The same thought is picked up in 1 Pet. 1.15: 'as he who called you is holy, be holy yourselves in all your conduct'. God's holiness cannot be isolated from God's calling of a people. God's holiness is actual as election to covenant, an election which is ever renewed in God's acts of judgement and reconciliation:

> The holy God . . . acts as the one who elects, *the one who draws to himself,* the one who establishes fellowship – as the one who brings salvation and gives himself . . . The wholly Other of the divine holiness finds its most potent expression in the reality that fellowship with him is only possible on the basis of the fact that out of himself and in free love he took to himself the enslaved Israelite tribes.[32]

This unbreakable link between holiness and covenant is crucial, because it articulates how God's holiness is not an abstract and oppositional attribute but a relational one, the ground of the free and merciful relation of the righteous God to his people.

The holiness of the covenant-creating God cannot be expounded as if it were simply a kind of moral purity that keeps itself aloof from all pollution. There is certainly a half-truth in this notion: moral purity involves separation; there can be no easy fellowship between God and wickedness (and therefore between God's people and wickedness); God's holiness means that he is 'of purer eyes than to behold evil, and canst not look on wrong' (Hab. 1.13). But the half-truth can become a distortion if we fail to see that God's holiness is much more than rectitude in conformity with an abstract moral law. In his *Lectures on the Philosophical Doctrine of Religion* from the first half of the 1780s, Kant remarks that '[r]eason leads us to God as holy legislator,' for '[h]oliness is the absolute or unlimited moral perfection of the will. A holy being must not be affected with the least inclination contrary to morality . . . So under-

stood, no being but God is holy.'[33] But Kant radically mis-
construes the dynamic of divine holiness. Partly this is because
he makes God into a mere instance of congruity with a moral
law external to his being, rather than seeing God as in himself
'the fountain of all holiness'.[34] But it is also because he fails to
see that God's holiness is not primarily morally legislative but
soteriological. The dynamic of holiness is that of the history of
God's saving, consecrating presence; holiness as 'law' makes
sense only in the commonwealth of salvation which that presence establishes. And so, once again, God's utter separation
from wickedness is to be understood within the scope of God's
dealings with humankind. Holiness is not the antithesis of
relation – it does not drive God from the unholy and lock God
into absolute pure separateness. Rather, God's holiness is the
quality of God's relation to that which is unholy; as the Holy
One, God is the one who does not simply remain in separation
but comes to his people and purifies them, making them into his
own possession. Talk of God's holiness indicates the manner in
which the sovereign God *relates*. As the Holy One, God passes
judgement on sin and negates it. Yet the holy God does this,
not from afar, as a detached legislator, but in the reconciling
mission of the Son and the outpouring of the sanctifying Spirit.
That is, God's destruction of sin is accomplished in his triune
acts of *fellowship* with humanity, in which he condemns,
pardons and cleanses by taking upon himself the situation of the
ruined creature, in sovereign majesty exposing himself to our
peril and only in that way putting an end to our unholiness.
God's 'active opposition to sin' is thus known in the economy of
salvation as a 'unity of judgement and grace'.[35]

It is at just this point that a Christian theological account of
the holiness of God will move into discussion of the trinitarian
nature of God. The doctrine of the Trinity tells us who God is on
the basis of God's works of creation, salvation and perfection.

As such, it is a crucial blockage against a temptation to which all theologies are exposed, namely, that of cramping or truncating the scope of God's relation to the world, and identifying God with only one mode of relation. On a trinitarian account of the matter, talk of the holiness of God indicates the relation of God to the world which we can discern in the full sweep of his works. Above all, the doctrine of the Trinity prevents abstract accounts of God's holiness – 'abstract' in the sense of being developed apart from attention to the identity of God which is enacted in his threefold repetition of himself in the economy of salvation as Father, Son and Spirit. Thus as Father, God is the one who wills and purposes from all eternity the separation of humankind as a holy people, destined for fellowship with himself. As Son, God is the one who achieves this separation of humankind by rescuing humanity from its pollution and bondage to unholiness. As Spirit, God is the one who completes or perfects that separation by sanctifying humankind and drawing it into righteous fellowship with the holy God. Only such a trinitarian account of the holiness of God can do real justice to the character of divine holiness in its relational character as that which elects, separates and purifies. In effect, what the doctrine of the Trinity does in this context is articulate how God's holiness is known in his covenant-creating and covenant-sustaining acts. Isaiah repeatedly puts together the ideas of God as the Holy One and God as Redeemer and Saviour (Isa. 41.14; 43.3; 48.17; 49.7): 'your Redeemer is the Holy One of Israel'. God's holiness is precisely that which is made known in his mercy, in his coming to the aid of his people, in his taking up their cause, in his bearing their sin, in his purifying of them and in his binding them to his own life.

All this, in short, is what is meant by the statement: As Father, Son and Spirit, God is the Holy One in our midst, establishing, maintaining and perfecting righteous fellowship with the holy

people of God. This is what might be termed 'positive' divine
holiness – holiness in its sanctifying aspect. It is within this context that we may most fittingly proceed to discuss what can be
termed 'negative' holiness, that is, holiness as a purity which is
destructive of wickedness. God's holiness is the undeflected
purposiveness with which God ensures that his will for
humankind will not be spoiled by wickedness. As the Holy One,
the triune God is at work to ensure that the end of the human
creature – what we have called 'righteous fellowship with God' –
will be attained, and sin will not be allowed to lead to the creature's ruin and destruction. God's holiness is thus inseparable
from his covenant faithfulness – his undefeated determination
that the creature will flourish and reach its end. Part of that
determination is the opposition of God's holiness to that which
is unholy. The unholy is that which lies beyond the will of God.
The unholy is the absurd affair in which the creature seeks to be
creature in a way other than that which is purposed by God; it is,
therefore, a way in which the creature – precisely by trying to
cease to be a creature and to make itself – seeks to destroy itself.
To this unholiness the holiness of God is implacably opposed. looks like?
But we may not isolate this moment of opposition; we may not
extract it from the larger scope of God's dealings with
humankind and make it into the only feature of the landscape.
To do that would be to miss the real point of talk of God's holiness by making it into some theoretical or abstract principle
standing in opposition to unholiness, and to fail to see the true
end of this negative aspect of God's holiness. To think of God's
holiness in such terms would be to fail to trace the history of
holiness in relation. In that history, God's holiness figures itself
as the righteous will of the Father for the creature, which is
embodied in the Son's work of sin-bearing and reconciliation,
and extended into us in the Spirit's consecration of the reconciled. And it is by that history – not by any general, impersonal

concepts of inviolable sanctity – that holy reason is to be instructed in the matter of the holiness of God. God's negative holiness is the destructive energy of God's positive holiness; it is the holiness of the triune God who – precisely because he wills to sustain the creature – must obliterate everything which thwarts the creature's life with God. God's holiness destroys wickedness for the same reason that we human beings destroy disease: because it attacks the creature's flourishing and is opposed to our well-being. And as the end of the eradication of disease is health, so the end of the eradication of unholiness is the creature's consecration, that is, the creature's wholesome life in righteous fellowship with God.

It is in this connection that we are to understand, therefore, the link between God's holiness and God's jealousy. 'I the Lord your God am a jealous God' (Ex. 20.5). It is rather easy to fall into a trap as dogmatics tries to make a conceptual paraphrase of what is being confessed here. Talk of the divine jealousy can project an idolatrous representation of God as a magisterial figure with a considerable sense of his own dignity, one whose self-love is easily wounded; or it can suggest that God is jealous like a wilful child, seeking to possess and control the whole world. But God's jealousy is not such, because it is the jealousy of the Holy Trinity. The jealousy of God is certainly what Brunner calls 'an active self-differentiation, the willed energy with which God asserts and maintains the fact that He is Wholly Other against all else'.[36] But this 'willed energy' of God is not some aseity apart from his directedness to the creature's cause. It is precisely the energy of the will with which God directs himself in all his works and ways towards us. The jealousy of the triune God is his purposiveness. It is his refusal to negotiate away the creature's good by allowing the creature itself to set the terms on which it will live. Certainly, God's jealousy is God's fierce opposition to all that thwarts God's will; as the jealous

God, God overcomes, and none may stand in his path. But this jealous holiness, precisely in its opposition to and destructiveness of our wickedness, is that which ensures our flourishing. Ezekiel puts it thus: 'I will restore the fortunes of Jacob, and have mercy upon the whole house of Israel; and I will be jealous for my holy name' (Ezek. 39.25). God's jealousy is his holiness in his work of restoration and mercy, as we are cleansed by the blood of Jesus (1 Jn 1.7) and sanctified by the washing of regeneration and renewal in the Holy Spirit (Tit. 3.5). Just because 'God's holiness is his sheer otherness, his sheer difference from everything else . . . it expresses itself . . . positively in his establishing of the goodness of the creature that is other than he'.[37]

We may draw these threads together by giving a more explicit trinitarian statement of what has been suggested so far about the inseparability of Trinity, holiness and covenant. The Holy Trinity is made known in the work of redeeming and consecrating a holy people. The holy God is God *with* us, God *for* us. In trinitarian terms, this comes out something like this: God the holy Father is the one who wills a people for himself. The Father's holiness is thus his work of purposing a people for himself, of securing from all eternity that what Israel and the Church signify will be established, namely, creatures in fellowship with God. The God and Father of our Lord Jesus Christ, Ephesians tells us, 'chose us in him before the foundation of the world, that we should be holy and blameless before him' (Eph. 1.4). God the holy Son is the one who condescends to turn to the world in grace as its saviour and redeemer. The Son's holiness is thus his work of rescuing those whom the Father wills for fellowship with himself. It is the merciful friendship with which he comes to the aid of sick and sinful and polluted humanity. It is the holy fellowship in which he takes our place, bears the burden of our sins, and releases us from their contamination. As the Son, the holy God embodies his mercy, redeeming Israel and the Church

and, in them, humankind from the threat of sin, remaking what
1 Peter calls 'a holy nation, God's own people' (1 Pet. 2.9). The
work of the Son is thus to reconcile us and present us 'holy and
blameless and irreproachable' before the Father (Col. 1.22). God
the Holy Spirit is the one who completes this work of making
holy, perfecting the creature by binding the creature's life into
that of Christ and so realizing *in* the creature what has been
achieved *for* the creature. The Spirit's holiness is thus known in
his work of sanctifying. As Paul puts it in 1 Corinthians, 'you
were washed, you were sanctified . . . in the name of the Lord
Jesus and in the Spirit of our God' (1 Cor. 6.11). Who, then, is the
holy God? For the Christian confession, he is this one: the thrice
Holy One, worshipped in the Apocalypse and in the prayers of
the Church thus:

> Holy, holy, holy, is the Lord God Almighty,
> who was and is and is to come! (Rev. 4.8)

Theology as the exercise of holy reason is a paraphrase of that
cry of praise.

That paraphrase cannot be completed, however, without
reflection on the work of God in the creatures who give voice to
God's holiness. To round out this trinitarian account of God's
holiness, we will follow through the movement of the communication of God's holiness to the communion of saints, both in
their common life and in their individual lives. '[I]t is fit', says
Jonathan Edwards, that 'as there is an infinite fountain of
holiness, moral excellence and beauty, so it should flow out in
communicated holiness'.[38] To that lofty matter, we shall give
ourselves in the next chapter.

3

The Holiness of the Church

I

The previous chapter sketched an account of a trinitarian dogmatics of the holiness of God. Central to the account was the
claim that God's holiness is a mode of his relation to his
creation: the holiness of the Holy Trinity is made known as God
speaks his holy name and, in majestic freedom, accomplishes his
work as creator, reconciler and perfecter. Holiness is one of the
ways of characterizing the covenant-creating and covenant-
sustaining presence of the glorious three-in-one. Because of this
– because holiness is known in God's movement towards us as
the creative Father, as the reconciling Son who is for us even
when in his righteousness he is opposed to our sin, and as the
consecrating Spirit – an account of the holiness of God is in-
complete without attention to the creatures before whom God
is sanctifyingly present. It is a fundamental rule of Christian
theology that a doctrine of God which is *only* a doctrine of God
is not a Christian doctrine of God. The task of articulating a
Christian doctrine of God, because it is a doctrine of the Holy
Trinity made known in free majesty in the economy of creation,
reconciliation and perfection, is not finished when it has spoken
of God in himself (*in se*); for God is essentially, to the depths of
his triune being, God for us and God with us, the one whose
mercy evokes the miracle of human fellowship with himself.

There is always a double theme in Christian theology, a twofold-ness in all its matter which corresponds to the identity of aseity and self-giving in the life of the Holy Trinity.

In terms of giving a dogmatic account of the holiness of God, this means that to the treatment of God's holiness there neces-sarily belongs a treatment of the holiness of the saints, that is, the holiness of the Church as the *sanctorum communio,* and the holiness of the individual Christian, who is a 'saint in Christ Jesus' (Phil. 4.21). The next two chapters will be given over to a description of this theme, looking first at the Church as the communion of saints and then at the believer's life of sancti-fication.

II

To begin with, however, we need to ask a question which, at first glance, seems purely formal or procedural, but which in fact takes us quickly to the heart of some central substantive issues. The question is this: How do we move from the doctrine of God to the doctrine of the Church? In what precise way are theology proper and ecclesiology to be related? That there is, indeed, such a relation, and that it is constitutive for theological talk about the nature of the Church, is the burden of a good deal of recent trinitarian theology, especially those styles of social trinitarian thought which emphasize that the Holy Trinity is to be con-ceived as a society of persons not only constituted by their per-sonal relations but overflowing in gracious relation to the human community of the Church. The resourcefulness of social trinitarianism for our understanding of human common life, both politically and in the Church, has been a matter of much emphasis. The relatedness of Father, Son and Spirit is canvassed as the ground or model for the Church, and the Church is thereby conceived as the realization in time of the human vocation to society, and so as the social extension of reconciliation through its gracious participation in the triune life of God. Much might be said in response to this aspect of social trinitarian theologies, but for our purposes two initial hesitations might be recorded.

The first is that such accounts of the life of the Church as a participation in or image of the relatedness of God characteristically give insufficient attention to the free majesty of God. The gracious or miraculous character of the Church, its sheer difference over against the perfect work of God which brings it into being, is often in some measure compromised by the easy, unproblematic way in which the language of participation is often deployed. The Hegelian cast of much modern ecclesiology is very much in evidence, and meets little resistance from those who interleave ecclesiology and the doctrine of God.

A second, related, hesitation concerns the way in which such accounts of the Church's relation to the triune life of God betray a drift into divine immanence. This can be seen in the way in which such ecclesiologies characteristically stress the continuity between the action of God and the action of the Church, in a manner which can easily jeopardize our sense of the freedom and perfection of God's work. Such ecclesiologies can place excessive emphasis upon the Church as agent, and, correspondingly, underplay the passivity which is at the heart of the Church as a creature of divine grace. For if the being of the Church is a participation in the life of the triune divine society, then it is in the work of the Church that the work of the triune God finds its realization and, in an important sense, its continuation. In effect, this constitutes an orientation in ecclesiology that makes the work of the Church an actualization of or sharing in the divine presence and action, rather than a testimony to that presence and action. In short: the repeated *hapax* ('once') of Heb. 9.26–28 – the uniqueness, the utter fullness, perfection and

sufficiency of the work of Father, Son and Spirit – is to some
degree endangered when the Church is considered to enter into
the movement of the divine work. One result of this is that the
holiness of the Church is no longer sheerly alien, no longer the
result of the Word's declaration, but in some sense infused into
the Church by the Church's *koinonia* with God, its perichoretic
relation to the Holy Trinity.

The account that I want to offer here of the relation between
the doctrine of the Trinity and the doctrine of the Church's holiness is of a quite different complexion. Above all, this is because
it makes the miracle of election central to the Church's existence
and nature. Where the social trinitarian language of participation emphasizes the continuity, even coinherence, of divine and
ecclesial action, the language of election draws attention to the
way in which the Church has its being in the ever-fresh work of
divine grace. The Church is what it is in the ceaseless gift of its
being through the risen Christ and the Holy Spirit who accomplish the will of the Father in gathering a holy people to himself.
Only thus, I want to suggest, can we retain the wisdom of
speaking of the Church's sanctity as an *alien* sanctity, a non-
possessable holiness. However, a caution needs to be entered
lest, in countering the Hegelian tendencies of social trinitarian
ecclesiologies, we overreact and bifurcate God and the Church.
It is, doubtless, true that the alien character of the Church – its
sheer difference from God – can be so stressed that the ecclesiology which results is spiritualized and dualist: spiritualized, in
the sense that we lose sight of the Church as human historical
society, dualist in the sense that it polarizes God and the human
community and renders God as a purely transcendent reality,
unrelated to human social space and time. The counter to those
dangers, however, is not to erode the distinction between God
and the human historical reality of the Church – to deal with the
dangers in that way would not be to solve, but simply to repeat,

the problem. Rather, the most effective counter is to offer a disciplined theological description of the nature and acts of the holy Church: that is, to govern our thinking in this matter by the gospel. Gospel discipline will require us to say both that the Church's holiness is real and actual, a perceptible form of common human being and action, and also that the being and action of the Church are holy only in so far as they have within themselves a primary reference to the work and word of the holy God. The Church is holy; but it is holy, not by virtue of some ontological participation in the divine holiness, but by virtue of its calling by God, its reception of the divine benefits, and its obedience of faith. Like its unity, its catholicity and its apostolicity, the Church's holiness is that which it is by virtue of its sheer contingency upon the mercy of God.

III

To expand on this in more detail we discuss, first, the *grounds* of the Church's holiness. In propositional form:

The holiness of the Church is grounded in the work of the Holy Trinity in electing, reconciling and perfecting a people to become God's covenant partners and the fellowship of the saints.

What is meant here?

There is a Church. Within the ambiguous kingdom of human time and society there exists an assembly, a congregation of men and women who constitute the covenant people and the fellowship of the saints. Their common life is the sign that there is, indeed, a human response to the divine call; to the divine self-utterance – 'I shall be your God' – there really does correspond a human reality, the gathering of God's people. But the existence

of such a gathering is wholly astonishing. It is grounded in no
human possibility; indeed, from the side of human history it is
nothing other than a sheer impossibility, for the commonwealth
of human time lies under the sway of sin and alienation, striving
with all its might to oppose God and to refuse his call to reconciliation. Apart from God, human history is populated by that
bleak, estranged and ruined company called 'no people' (1 Pet.
2.10: *ou laos*; cf. Hos. 2.23). But ingredient within the gospel confession is the claim that there now exists the extraordinary fact
of *laos theou*, people of God. There is a form of common human
life which can only be described as a holy nation, a people for
God's possession (1 Pet. 2.9). That such a holy people exists and
is preserved through time, that it does not collapse back into
alienation and hatred, that here sin is held in check and not
permitted to eat away at human fellowship – all this lies in the
hands of the holy God alone.

Put in more formal dogmatic terms: all talk of the Church's
holiness is rooted in talk of the holiness of God. He, the holy
three-in-one, what he is and what he does, is the ground of the
Church's existence and of its endurance. Language about God is
to be *operative* language in talking of the grounds of the holiness
of the Church: in giving an account of the entirety of its history
and of all its activity, including its holiness, this language about
God is of critical significance. God is not merely the Church's
initial cause nor its remote end; rather, the Church is because
God is. The Church is holy because God is holy. And therefore
the *sanctitas ecclesiae* is at heart *sanctitas passiva*, a matter of
faith's trustful reliance upon and reference to the work of the
triune God:

> In respect of its holiness the community is bound to [Christ]
> ... only to the extent that He constantly wills to bind Himself
> and does in fact bind Himself to it. He is always the Subject,

the Lord, the Giver of the holiness of its action. Its action as such can only be a seeking, an asking after holiness, a prayer for it.[1]

Why, we might ask, is it that the *triune* God is the ground of the Church's holiness? For an answer, we might pause a little to look at the elaboration of this point in that magisterial declaration of proto-trinitarian theology, the letter to the Ephesians.[2] There, the holiness of the Church is grounded, first, in the electing activity of the Father. 'Blessed be the God and Father of our Lord Jesus Christ, who has blessed us in Christ with every spiritual blessing . . . , even as he chose us in him before the foundation of the world, that we should be holy and blameless before him' (Eph. 1.3–4). Viewed in the context of the overall scope of the first chapter of the letter, this statement in these early verses can be seen as conveying a double affirmation: that the ground of holiness is election, and that the goal of election is holiness. If there exists a human realm of holiness, if holiness has an enduring human and social form, then that form is to be traced to its generative source in the electing activity of the God and Father of our Lord Jesus, condensed into the single word: *exelexato* – he chose. But alongside this: if there is an election of grace, then it is no mere self-enclosed divine movement, but a moving power in human history, that which has as its *telos* the recreation of a holy people of God, bound to him as the echo of and testimony to his own proper holiness. Election and sanctification, in other words, are inseparably linked.[3] As Calvin puts it: 'God's eternal election is the foundation and first cause both of our calling and of all the benefits which we have received from God . . . holiness, innocence, and every virtue in men, are the fruit of election . . . all our holiness and innocence of life flow from the election of God.'[4] And though the 'chief design' of election is 'the glory of God', there is for Calvin, nevertheless, an important immediate or subordinate design of the Father's electing activity, namely, 'our sanctification'.[5]

Already an important consequence for our understanding of the Church's holiness begins to emerge. The dynamic of the Church's holiness is not that of natural separation and association, but of election, segregation and assembly by God. The holy people of God is a form of common life which owes its origin to a decision and act beyond itself, utterly gratuitous, excluding from consideration 'everything which men have of themselves'.[6] Neither in its origin nor in its continuation is the sanctified community an autonomous gathering; it is – at every moment of its existence – a creature of grace. The dynamic of its life is, therefore, in no sense self-generated. God separates the Church. The Church does not separate itself, for it has neither mandate nor competence to do so; indeed, to try to do so is blasphemy, for it is to try to repeat by a human action the work of election which is God's alone. The Church's holiness is the result of the divine decision, not of any human acts of separating a 'pure' group from an 'impure'. In this respect, the true holiness of the Church is very different indeed from purely human social sectarianism, and readings either of the Churches of the New Testament era or of contemporary Christianity that view holiness merely as a sociological or ethnographic quantity miss the point.[7] Only God is properly holy; only God may elect the Church; only an elect Church is sanctified. The Church's holiness is thus grounded in the election of God the Father.

Second, the Church's holiness which is the goal or 'subordinate design' of election is established in the reconciling work of the Son, who cleansed the Church that it might be holy. '[Christ] loved the Church and gave himself up for her, that he might sanctify her, having cleansed her by the washing of water with the word, that he might present the Church to himself in splendour, without spot or wrinkle or any such thing, that she might be holy and without blemish' (Eph. 5.25–27; see also 1 Cor. 1.2; Phil. 1.1). The Father's will, we have already been told in Ephesians 1, is effected in the Son who 'sets forth' (Eph. 1.9) the purpose of the Father. If we ask how the sanctifying purpose of the Father is effected in the Son, Ephesians gives us a range of concepts: redemption (Eph. 1.7); forgiveness of trespasses (Eph. 1.7); being brought near (Eph. 2.13); sacrifice (Eph. 5.2) and, near the end of Ephesians 5, cleansing (Eph. 5.26). Here the metaphor of cleansing recapitulates the entirety of Christ's saving work: the objective work of Jesus Christ in his death and resurrection, which is the divine act of defeating sin and putting an end to its pollution of humankind; and the applicative work of Jesus Christ in 'the washing of water with the word', that is, in baptism and the gospel's word of promise. That work, moreover, is teleological – unique, unrepeatable, imparticipable, but nevertheless a work which evokes a human trajectory, a social form. Baptism, Calvin remarks, has an 'aim'; and the aim is twofold: separation or what we might call 'passive sanctification' (of which the outward sign is baptism, as the visible confirmation of God's promise), and 'active sanctification', for the end of baptism is 'that we may live holy and unblameable to God'.[8]

Third, the Church's holiness which is the goal of election and which is established in the reconciling work of the Son is perfected by the Holy Spirit. Through the work of the Spirit, the Church, elect and cleansed, is made into a dwelling place of God: the Church 'is joined together and grows into a holy temple in the Lord; in whom you also are built into it for a dwelling place of God in the Spirit' (Eph. 2.21–22). The work of the Spirit is to 'perfect', that is, to bring to completion or full realization the reality which is willed in election and established in reconciliation. The Spirit is God himself consummating the design of reconciliation, whose goal is that there should be covenant fellowship between himself and the creatures whom he has made and redeemed by drawing them into relation with himself. The language here – 'reconciliation,' 'fellowship', 'relation' – is deliberate: it is not the language of participation. 'In the Lord' and 'in the Spirit' do not mean union of being between God and the Church. Their reference is not to ontological communion but to soteriology and its fruits; they indicate the saving divine agency which creates and recreates fellowship between God and his creatures, anticipated in the Church which is God's 'dwelling place', that is, a form of common life in which the restoration of the covenant is at work. The *telos* of the work of the Son is ending alienation (Eph. 2.12), breaking down the wall of hostility both within the human realm (between Jew and Gentile) and vertically, by reconciliation to God (Eph. 2.16). That work of reconciliation is pointed to its completion – though not, of course, completed here and now – by the Spirit, who not only effects a renewed relation to God the Father (Eph. 2.18: 'we both have access in one Spirit to the Father'), but also renews human fellowship, making us into 'fellow citizens with the saints' (Eph. 2.19). Crucially, the completion of the work of the Church's sanctification is not an undertaking of the Church itself; the repetition of 'through the Spirit' at the end of Ephesians 2, Calvin says, is partly 'to remind them that all human powers are of no avail without the operation of the Spirit'.[9] In sum: If there exists a covenant people and a communion of saints – if the will of the Father to dwell with humankind is effected, if the reconciling work of the Son is realized in human life and history in a body or form of common life – then it is because the Church exists 'in the Spirit', by the Spirit's agency and by the ever-fresh coming of the Spirit, in the realm of transformation in which the Spirit is Lord.

So far, then, I have suggested that the ground of the holiness of the Church is the saving work of the Holy Trinity. The Church's holiness is therefore an *alien* sanctity. Because the

Church is holy by grace, and because grace is a movement of relation and not a mere handing over of a commodity, then in the case of the Church the attribution of holiness is not a matter of the straightforward ascription of a property. God's holiness is proper to him; indeed, it *is* him, for he is originally holy. The holiness of the Church, by contrast, is not a natural or cultural condition. As with all the predicates of the Church, the Church is what it is *spiritually*, that is, by virtue of the presence and action of the triune God. This is an application in the matter of holiness of the great ontological rule for the Church which is announced in Eph. 2.8–10: 'By grace you have been saved through faith; and this is not your own doing, it is the gift of God – not because of works, lest any man should boast. For we are his workmanship, created in Christ Jesus for good works, which God prepared beforehand, that we should walk in them.' There we have in brief compass what needs to be said about the ontology of the Church. The Church is what it is by grace. This entails a denial that the agency at the heart of the Church is the Church's own spontaneity: 'not your own doing . . . not because of works'. And it entails an affirmation that the agency at the heart of the Church is God's, for the Church is 'God's workmanship, created in Christ Jesus'. There is, accordingly, a proper passivity to the being of the Church, for *faith* – that is, recognition and assent and trust in the word and work of God – and not *boasting* – that is, self-grounded, proud competence – is the fundamental act of the Church's existence. From this ontological rule about the holy Church's constitution there follows a further rule about the action of the holy Church: all the acts of the holy Church must demonstrate a reference to the work of the One who alone is holy: the electing Father who reconciles in the Son and perfects in the Spirit.

Next, therefore, we move to look at the *practices of holiness*. What human and social form is taken by this reference to the

work of the holy God? How do faith and the absence of boasting
become a mode of common life? To answer this, we move to the
next proposition which reads:

> *The holiness of the Church is visible in all its acts as confession of*
> *the name of God, the thrice Holy One, the Lord of hosts.*

IV

As we looked at the ground of the Church's holiness, our thinking was both guided by and directed towards a biblical text; in
looking at the matter of the practices of holiness, our thinking
may helpfully be instructed by a non-biblical text of great
antiquity and endurance in the tradition of the Church's worship, namely, the ancient Christian hymn usually entitled *Te
Deum Laudamus.* This hymn is sometimes called the 'Canticle
of Ambrose and Augustine', from the legend that at the baptism
of Augustine by Ambrose the hymn was improvised and sung
alternately by the two saints. Probably of late-fourth-century
origin, it found its way into Western liturgy as a canticle at
the end of the night office, and was incorporated into mattins in
the Sarum Breviary and thence into the Reformation Anglican
Book of Common Prayer, where it remains as one of the minor
treasures of Anglican public worship. The canticle runs thus:

> We praise thee, O God : we acknowledge thee to be the Lord.
> All the earth doth worship thee : the Father everlasting.
> To thee all Angels cry aloud : the Heavens, and all the Powers
>   therein.
> To thee Cherubim, and Seraphim : continually do cry,
> Holy, Holy, Holy : Lord God of Sabaoth;
> Heaven and earth are full of the Majesty : of thy Glory.

The glorious company of the Apostles : praise thee.

The goodly fellowship of the Prophets : praise thee.

The noble army of Martyrs : praise thee.

The holy Church throughout all the world : doth acknowledge thee;

The Father : of an infinite Majesty;

Thine honourable, true : and only Son;

Also the Holy Ghost : the Comforter.

Thou art the King of Glory : O Christ.

Thou art the everlasting Son : of the Father.

When thou tookest upon thee to deliver man : thou didst not abhor the Virgin's womb.

When thou hadst overcome the sharpness of death : thou didst open the Kingdom of Heaven to all believers.

Thou sittest at the right hand of God : in the Glory of the Father.

We believe that thou shalt come : to be our Judge.

We therefore pray thee, help thy servants : whom thou hast redeemed with thy precious blood.

Make them to be numbered with thy Saints : in glory everlasting.

O Lord, save thy people : and bless thine heritage.

Govern them : and lift them up for ever.

Day by day : we magnify thee;

And we worship thy Name : ever world without end.

Vouchsafe, O Lord : to keep us this day without sin.

O Lord, have mercy upon us : have mercy upon us.

O Lord, let thy mercy lighten upon us : as our trust is in thee.

O Lord, in thee have I trusted : let me never be confounded.

It is a lofty text for speaking the praises of almighty God, especially in those repeated glorious Latin vocatives (*Te* . . .) at the beginning of the lines (lost, sadly, in the English rendering), which thrust the worshipper towards the supreme grandeur of God, the 'Thou' who is the centre of Christian praise. The hymn falls into three parts: an act of homage to the Holy Trinity; a recital of the saving work of Christ; and a set of prayers to Christ, asking that he will come to the aid of his people. At its centre, we find this said of the work of the holy Church:

> The holy Church throughout all the world : doth acknow-
>   ledge thee;
> The Father : of an infinite Majesty;
> Thine honourable, true : and only Son;
> Also the Holy Ghost : the Comforter.

It is this act – the act of acknowledging or, perhaps better, confessing (*confiteor*) the holy God, this echoing of the unceasing cry of the cherubim and seraphim – which, I suggest, is the fundamental act of the holy Church. In that act is manifest the basic character of the Church's holiness, for, in the act of confession, the Church joins with the prophets and apostles and martyrs, all those whose lives have been transfigured by the divine calling, and becomes that human company which is holy in its confession of this one, the Lord God of hosts.

To expand our reflections on this, we address three questions:

(1) What is it about confession or acknowledgement that makes it basic to the Church's holiness?

(2) What is it that the holy Church acknowledges in making its confession of the triune God?

(3) In what practices of confession is the Church's holiness visible?

(1) *What is it about confession or acknowledgement that makes it basic to the Church's holiness?* 'We praise thee, O God: we

acknowledge thee to be the Lord . . . The holy Church throughout all the world: doth acknowledge thee . . .'. Confession or acknowledgment is *recognition*. It is an action in which the worth, dignity and goodness of that which is other than the Church is accorded the recognition of which it is supremely deserving. In confession, the Church simply assents to God's reality, uttering its 'Amen' to God's manifest being and works: 'Blessed be the Lord for ever! Amen and Amen' (Ps. 89.52). Confession in this sense is not an isolated or discrete activity in the Church's existence. Rather, in the entirety of its being and in all its activities, the Church acts out the basic structure of confession – it celebrates in all it is and does the fact that it is the creature of God's mercy. Because of this, the Church's holiness, too, is at its heart a confession. Holiness, we have seen, is not a static property of the Church but a movement or event. That movement, the history that we call the Church's holiness, is a twofold movement, or, perhaps better, a commerce between two unequal realities. The history of the Church's holiness includes as a first and primary movement the condescension of the holy God who mercifully elects, assembles and consecrates the *communio sanctorum*. And it includes as a secondary and derivative movement the congregation of the saints, evoked by God's mercy, among whom and by whom the holiness of Father, Son and Spirit is confessed. The Church's holiness – again like its unity, catholicity and apostolicity – occurs as part of this history of grace and confession. The Church is holy, that is, as it cries to God: 'holy, holy, holy, Lord God of hosts'.

This acknowledgement originates, of course, in God himself. The Church cannot confess unless God opens its mouth. Confession takes its rise, not in the Church, but in God's manifestation of himself as the Holy One, in God's communicative presence as revealer. Revelation is enacted and declared salvation, the visible hand of the holy and merciful Trinity. And revelation generates the communion of saints, the gathering of those called to holiness in fellowship with the everlasting Father, the eternal Son and the Spirit of consolation. Only on the basis of this divine vocation and enabling is it possible for the people of God to say: *Te Deum laudamus.*

(2) *What is it that the holy Church acknowledges in making its confession of the triune God?* The holy Church acknowledges God. The God who is acknowledged in this way is the active subject of the work of salvation. He is the Father of infinite majesty; the true and only Son, worthy of all worship; the Holy Spirit, the comforter – the three-in-one manifest in the divine work of delivering humankind from the bondage of sin. And the Church fulfils the goal of its consecration by God when it confesses this work. In doing so, it joins in the worship which the entire creation offers; hence in the *Te Deum* we are given a series of statements ascending from earth to the heavenly throne of God: 'All the earth doth worship thee . . . To thee all angels cry aloud . . . the heavens and all the powers . . . cherubim and seraphim' – all these separate praises combine into the great confessional (and theological, and metaphysical) cry: 'Heaven and earth are full of the majesty of thy glory!'

In a little more detail: the holy Church acknowledges the *Father* of infinite majesty. God's majesty as Father is the supreme eminence of his being, will and works, a majesty which is limitless in extent, uncontainable, without measure or circumspection, always and everywhere utterly replete. This infinite majesty is not an isolated attribute; it is, rather, a property of the divine essence which characterizes all that God is. And so God's holiness, too, is inseparable from his majesty; and this is why the holy Church invokes the Father of infinite majesty by crying: 'Holy!'

The holy Church acknowledges the true and only *Son*, worthy of all worship. The *Te Deum* in its entirety is characterized by an exalted Christology, especially in its recital of the Son's work of condescension and exaltation, so that over the whole hymn stand the words at the beginning of the second section: *Tu rex gloriae Christe*. Here, in the statement of the Holy Trinity as the object of the Church's praises, the focus is on the person who accomplishes and is manifest in that work. This one is confessed as *truly* the Son of God – not Son by adoption, in no sense an annexe to the life of God, but himself ingredient within the divine identity, *vere Deus*, of one being with the Father and the Spirit. He is the *only* Son of God – the only-begotten, utterly unlike any creature, having an eternal origin, 'the everlasting Son of the Father', and therefore not *made*. And, being all this, he is accordingly 'worthy of all worship' (*venerandus*), for he shares in the dignity and glory of the godhead, and is fittingly the object of the devotion of heaven and earth.

This eternal glory of the Son is set forth in the accomplishment of the Son's mission in time. 'Glory' and 'mission' – the Son's eternal and transcendent majesty and his fulfilment in creaturely history of the will of the Father – are in the strictest way correlative. The Son is, in the confession of the holy Church, the king of glory, the Father's everlasting Son; and it is *as* this one (not *despite* the fact that he is this one) that he sets humankind free from sin and free for holiness. He submits to accomplish this work of deliverance, taking upon himself its ignominy, not shrinking from being born of a woman, and is pierced by the sting of death. And precisely because he does all this, his work is a work of *overcoming*: in it, he opens God's kingdom; having accomplished it, he is seated at the Father's right hand in glory, from whence he is awaited as judge of all things.

The holy Church acknowledges the *Holy Spirit*, the comforter. The Spirit only enters the recital of the object of the Church's praise at the end, and it would be easy enough to see this as typically Western pneumatological minimalism. Yet the reference to the Spirit is no mere appendage or afterthought; it is essential to the complete statement of the sweep of salvation history which the *Te Deum* celebrates. For the title 'Comforter' or 'Paraclete' gathers up into one word the fact that the Father and the Son would still be in some measure outside us if it were not for the fact that as Spirit, God undertakes to be present with his holy people for all time (Jn 14.16–17.). The Spirit is sent by the Father in the Son's name to instruct the saints by bearing witness to Christ (Jn 15.26). Indeed, without this third reference to the Spirit's perfecting work, the suffrages in the final section of the *Te Deum* ('We therefore pray thee, help thy servants . . .') would be a mere undirected cry, without secure hope of any answer. God's saving of his people, his blessing of his heritage, his governing and uplifting of the people of God, his keeping of his Church without sin, his preservation of the saints as holy – none of this would be possible without the confession of the Spirit's deity, without the third repetition of the cry: 'Holy!'

Let us now draw these threads together and indicate their connection to the Church's holiness. The Church is the communion of the saints as it confesses the name of God the thrice Holy One. God's name is God in his majestic self-manifestation as Lord and Saviour, the Holy One in our midst. As he utters his name and works his saving work, he creates and preserves for himself a people, set apart for his praise, consecrated to the work of acknowledging that God's name is holy, and so forming the modest human accompaniment to the confession of the heavenly powers: 'Holy, holy, holy is the Lord, the God of hosts.'

(3) *In what practices of confession is the Church's holiness visible?* What is the human, historical shape of holiness?

Initially, we need to probe the term 'visible' to ensure that we are using it in the right way. A good deal of mainstream modern ecclesiology (especially in its ecumenical versions) has been heavily committed to the visibility of the Church, that is, to the

Church's tangible, historical and material character as an ordered society. Corresponding to this commitment has been a consensus that the notion of the *in*visibility of the Church has little to commend it, because it suggests a spiritualizing of the Church into bare subjectivism without objective social form or durability. One result is that a high premium is placed on the externality of the Church, on the historical activity of the Church in which the Church's being is visible. Clearly there is a truth here: the Church is a real human assembly, known in its acts, and its holiness is therefore a visible phenomenon. But the key question is not *whether* the Church is visible but *what kind of visibility* it possesses. The visibility of the Church is not simply that of a natural quantity or life-force or social presence; it is the visibility of the 'invisible' Church – what Barth called its 'very special visibility'.[10] In speaking of this 'special visibility', Barth did not intend to deny that the Church always has historical concretion and form; he simply sought to affirm that the Church has such visible form by virtue of the presence and action of Christ through the Spirit. 'Visibility' is therefore a spiritual event. It is that which can be described only by talking of the active, communicative presence of the triune God. It cannot be converted into mere phenomenal form, and it can be fully perceived only by faith in the word and work of God. There is an immediate consequence of this for talk of the Church's *holiness.* The holiness of God's holy people is visible not simply as something predicated of the Church on the basis of its activities; to say this would be to convert holiness into something which the Church itself realized, and so to contradict the New Testament's witness that holiness is 'in Christ Jesus' (1 Cor. 1.2; Phil. 1.1). Rather, visible holiness is *confessed* of the Church; and that confession is not a recognition of a property which the Church has *in se*, but an acknowledgement of that which it is by virtue of the sovereign work of the triune God.

In the Church's practices of holiness, therefore, its action is
wholly oriented towards the action of the Holy Trinity, in electing, gathering and consecrating. The Church's acts do not
realize, complete, continue or in any way extend or embody
God's work, which is perfect, and which alone is properly holy.
The Church's acts of holiness, having their origin and their
sustaining energy in God, bear testimony to God's work,
accompanying it with their witness, and, in all their human
fragility and sinfulness, echoing the holy work of the holy God.
How does the holy Church act to accompany and echo the work
of God? Four things are to be said.

First, *the Church's holiness is visible as it hears afresh the
promise and command of the gospel.* Holiness occurs as the
Church submits once again to the gospel's judgement and consolation, its publication of salvation and its direction of the
people of God in the ways of holiness. The Church is holy as a
hearing Church.

Hearing the gospel is never a finished business, never something which the Church has behind it. It is always a fresh
activity, and so the Church's holiness is always a process of
the Church becoming holy by standing beneath the word of the
gospel as both *promise* and *command.* Standing beneath the
gospel's *promise* means hearing the joyful declaration: 'Behold
your God'. In such hearing the Church is once again faced with
the gospel's affirmation that God is one who comes, one who is
with us as saviour, renewing and preserving his people and
fulfilling with final authority the divine commitment: I will be
your God. The promise of the gospel is that 'the grace of God has
appeared for the salvation of all' (Tit. 2.11); that 'appearance' is
identical with 'our great God and Saviour Jesus Christ' (Tit.
2.13), the one who 'gave himself for us to redeem us from all
iniquity and to purify for himself a people of his own who are
zealous for good deeds' (Tit. 2.14). But to stand beneath that

promise of the gospel is already also to stand beneath the gospel's *commandment*: the end of God's work of purification is active zeal for good deeds. Thus the Church is also holy as it stands beneath the gospel's commandment. As commandment, the gospel is the declaration of the law, the shape or direction for the life of God's holy people. Hearing the gospel's summons to obedience, the Church is holy, submitting to the gospel's judgement of sin, and setting itself to govern its life by God's commands. In this way, the Church is holy as it stands beneath the final promulgation of the summons to that holiness which corresponds to the divine commitment of election: You shall be my people. How, then, is the Church holy? By attention and submission to the gospel as the indicative of election and the imperative of obedience.

Second, *the Church's holiness is visible as it confesses its sin in penitence and faith.* The Church is consecrated by the Father's resolve, holy in Christ and sanctified by the Holy Spirit. Such holiness is not achieved perfection, but an alien holiness which is the contradiction of its very real sinfulness. The Church is holy, not because it has already attained the eschatological state of being 'without spot or wrinkle', but because the promise and command of the gospel have already broken into its life and disturbed it, shaking it to the core. The Church is holy only as it is exposed to judgement.

This means that, far from being a matter of confident purity, holiness is visible as humble acknowledgement of sin and as prayer for forgiveness. 'There is no greater sinner than the Christian Church,' said Luther in his Easter Day sermon in 1531.[11] It is in repentance, rather than in the assumption of moral pre-eminence, that holiness is visible. Thus the Church's holiness is inseparable from its prayer (again, in the words of the *Te Deum*): 'O Lord have mercy upon us, have mercy upon us.' Realized moral excellence does not necessarily constitute holiness and may contradict it. Holiness is visible as faith's penitent cry for forgiveness and mercy, its appeal for God to do what the Church cannot do for itself, namely, to keep it without sin and to gather it into the company of the saints in glory.

Third, *the Church's holiness is visible as it bears witness to the world.* 'You are . . . a holy nation . . . that you may declare' (1 Pet. 2.9). The *origin* of the Church's holiness, as we have seen, is entirely outside itself; the consequences of this are that, first, it is manifest as a hearing of the gospel's promise and command, and, second, that its sign is penance, not perfection. Similarly, the *goal* of the Church's holiness lies beyond itself. The supreme end of the holiness of the Church is the glorification of God in the obedience of the saints; its intermediate goal is bearing witness. As the fellowship of the saints, the Church declares 'the wonderful deeds' of the one who has called the Church out of darkness into light, and so consecrated it for his service. Crucially, the dynamic of holiness includes not only gathering and withdrawal but also sending. The holiness of the saints is not a mere turning inwards; if it were, then it would all too quickly become mere sectarian hostility towards a profane world. If this kind of dynamic of withdrawal is questionable, it is not only because it tends to assume that the line between sin and achieved holiness coincides with the line between the Church and the world. It is also because strategies of withdrawal almost inevitably transpose the divine movement of election and consecration into social exclusivity, and so make the Church's holiness into a clean sphere over against a polluted world. It is precisely this transposition of holiness into the wrong kind of visibility that is one of the objects of Jesus' unsparing judgement. The real dynamic of visible holiness has a quite different character. There is, unquestionably, a radical separation, a 'calling out' which effects the Church's separation and which makes its members into a company of 'aliens and exiles'. And that separation is visible as 'abstinence', the Church's refusal to give itself to 'the passions of the flesh'. But the end of all this is 'that you may declare': holiness is to be maintained 'among the Gentiles' not simply to prevent the pollution of the Church, but with the end that 'they may see your good works and glorify God' (1 Pet. 2.12; cf. Mt. 5.16; Phil. 2.15). Holiness is visible as testimony, as good works which are transparent to and declare the wonderful deeds of the holy God.

Fourth, *the holiness of the Church is visible in its prayer: 'Hallowed be thy name!'* If the essence of holiness is confession of the Holy Trinity, then the primordial act in which holiness is visible is the Church's prayer that God's name be sanctified. That prayer is not, we must note, first and foremost a prayer that the Church itself somehow establish the sanctity of God's name. Quite the opposite: it is a prayer that God himself hallow his own name. As Barth suggests in his masterful unfinished exposition of the Lord's Prayer with which the *Church Dogmatics* broke off, the petition may be paraphrased thus:

> Father, do what thou alone canst do. See to it finally, perfectly, and definitively that thou and thy name are known . . . See to it that thy name is no longer desecrated but always and by everybody regarded as holy in the way that it is in fact holy as thy name that thou thyself has sanctified.[12]

Moreover, in praying this prayer, the holy Church is in an important sense looking backwards – back to the 'unique and definitive divine act which it knows to have taken place already in Jesus Christ . . . the unique and definitive act whereby God himself hallows his own name. This was and is already the end of all God's ways, the eschaton.'[13] The prayer of the Church, its trustful cry that in this matter God will take up his own cause and demonstrate his holiness, is thus rooted in 'the sanctifying of God's name by God himself'.[14] And so as it prays this prayer, the Church acts out the constitutive character of its holiness, namely, its indication of the holy name of God enacted in his deeds.

Yet in this indication the Church's holiness is no mere passive assent to a state of affairs – God's holiness – before which the Church can simply sit with folded hands. Certainly, this prayer is a prayer 'for an act that cannot be ours'.[15] But to God's self-sanctification there corresponds the holy Church's own acts of sanctifying God's name. For

> [t]hose who really press and involve God with this petition in the expectation that he will answer it, as people who are seriously and fundamentally disquieted and startled, press and involve themselves too in their own place and manner as people and within the limits of their own human capabilities and possibilities. They declare, and within their limits take on responsibility, that in the matter about which they pray to God something will be done correspondingly by them.[16]

We have already mentioned some of what might be involved in such holy action: hearing the gospel; testimony; and the sanctification of reason. But enclosing and undergirding all these works will be the work of praise. Praise is the great act of rebellion against sin, the great repudiation of our wicked refusal to acknowledge God to be the Lord. In sum, therefore: the Church is holy as, day by day, it magnifies God and worships his name, ever world without end.

4

The Holiness of the Christian

I

The attributes of God are ways of talking of the identity of the
triune God, and so, as we have seen, God's holiness is a trinitarian attribute, characterizing his life as Father, Son and Spirit.
The triune God's identity is enacted in the economy of creation,
reconciliation and perfection, in the work in which God is
creatively, savingly and communicatively present. God's holiness is thus a relational attribute, characterizing God's dealing
with that which he has made and redeems. To talk of the holiness of God is to summarize the being and works of the Holy
Trinity as God elects, redeems and completes holy fellowship
between himself and his people. This is why a dogmatic exposition of the holiness of God has to include within its scope an
account of the communication of holiness. This, not in the
sense of creaturely holiness as a participation in the triune being
of the holy God, nor in the sense of creaturely holiness as an
emanation of the divine, but in the sense of God's unceasing,
ever-fresh act of bestowing holiness upon the creature by the
creature's consecration. Communicated holiness is not trans-
ferred or possessed holiness, but derived holiness; and the
primary mark of creaturely holiness is thus its external orientation, its ordering towards God as its source and the object of its
praises.

So far in our sketch of the communication of holiness we have concentrated upon the common life of holiness, upon God's people as the *sanctorum communio*. But there is also a proper individuality to holiness, a propriety to giving a dogmatic account of the personal life of the Christian, the saint in Christ. As we shall come to see, this may not be done in such a way as to make the personal or subjective into the real centre around which all our language of the holy Church and the holy God orbits. To follow that path would not only subvert a proper sense that the holiness of the individual Christian occurs within the fellowship of God's holy people; it would also threaten to collapse the transcendent work of divine election, reconciliation and perfection into the little world of the individual saint. This kind of collapse has, of course, happened often enough in the history of the practice of piety and finds contemporary expression in some kinds of interest in spirituality as self-fulfilment. Nevertheless, the rule holds: *abusus non tollit usum*, abuse does not do away with proper use. There is a gospel legitimacy to talk of individual sanctity. For its exposition, all that is required is good dogmatic order, in which sanctity is rooted in an account of the ways of the Holy Trinity and has its context in the communion of the saints. Good dogmatic order will help promote good pastoral order, and so inhibit that inflammation of self-concern which can so afflict the life of piety and frustrate growth in holiness. In brief: what is needed is an orderly theological account of the individual Christian as 'sanctified in Christ Jesus' (1 Cor. 1.2). In propositional form, such an orderly account might be summarized thus:

The sanctification of the Christian is the work of the Holy Trinity in which the reconciled sinner is renewed for the active life of holy fellowship with God. Grounded in the electing, reconciling and perfecting work of Father, Son and Spirit, the active

life of holy fellowship is the work of faith, which is at every
moment characterized by mortification and vivification, and
which is actual as freedom, obedience and love.

II

First, then: *The sanctification of the Christian is the work of the*
Holy Trinity in which the reconciled sinner is renewed for the
active life of holy fellowship with God. Whence the miracle of the
Christian life? How does it come about that sin is overcome and
in its place there arises a new form of life which can be called
'holy'? How does it arise that a human life is set free from enmity
towards God, from disobedience and from hatred of neighbour,
and is restored to its proper ends? On what ground does the
active life of holy fellowship with God rest? The answer which
we must return is simply that the existence and continuation of
such a form of life and activity is grounded wholly in the sanctifying work of the Holy Trinity.

Sanctification is the Father's work of election. To say this is to
say that the active life of holy fellowship does not originate in
any human decision or determination, but rests on a divine
determination of utter gratuity and sovereign freedom. Sanctification is ingredient within the eternal resolve of God, and so
what was said of the Church must also be said of the individual
Christian: 'He chose us in him [Christ] before the foundation of
the world, that we should be holy' (Eph. 1.4). In talking of the
active life of holy fellowship, we are not in the sphere of human
decision. Our thinking about sanctification would be disorderly
if we were to suggest that, although in the matter of reconciliation we have to talk of a divine determination, when we move to
speak of human holiness we are required to shift to talk of our
own agency, perhaps co-operating with God, perhaps rendering

God his due in return for the gift of salvation. But, if we are elected to holiness, then we have been extracted from the sphere of human autonomy; the Christian's holiness does not stem from the Christian's decision. However, there is an important complementary truth here: election is election to a way of life. The condition of 'being elect' is not simply a state but a history; election to holiness is not merely segregation. Rather, election is determination, appointment to be and to act in a certain way. The movement of segregation is, certainly, indispensable, for consecration means difference. But segregation cannot be made absolute; what is established by God's election of grace is not a state, but the consecration of the sinner for active service of God:

> [P]ractice is the aim of that eternal election which is the first ground of the bestowment of all true grace. Good practice is not the ground of election . . . But Christian practice is the scope and end of election. Though God does not elect men because he foresees that they will live holy, yet he elects them that they may live holy.[1]

Sanctification is the Son's work of reconciliation. If we ask again the question: 'Whence the miracle of human holiness?', then alongside the answer that it has its origin in divine election we also have to say that sanctification is inseparable from God's reconciling work. The work of sanctification, resolved by the Father, is accomplished in the person and mission of the Son of God, the incarnate one, the strangely triumphant sin-bearer in whose blood we have redemption and the forgiveness of our trespasses. At its simplest: holiness rests on the foundation of forgiveness and reconciliation. This is what is meant by saying that the Christian is 'sanctified . . . in the name of the Lord Jesus Christ' (1 Cor. 6.11).

It has become customary in Protestant dogmatics and ethics

to secure this christological and soteriological point by insisting on a strictly sequential relationship between justification and sanctification: whatever is said about sanctification has to rest on the priority of the justifying work of Christ. Particularly in polemic against what were taken to be synergistic Roman Catholic accounts of the matter, the insistence upon rooting sanctification in justification through faith alone took to its full conclusion a sense of the radical character of God's saving grace. The move from justification to sanctification does not entail any compromise of the perfection and sufficiency of grace which is declared in the Word and assented to in faith. Sanctification rests on the divine act of salvation accomplished in the death and resurrection of the Son and pronounced in the gospel promulgation of acquittal. Consequently, the agent of Christian holiness is not the Christian but God. In effect, the rooting of sanctification in justification prohibits any conversion of sanctification into ethical self-improvement, as if justification were merely an initial infusion of capacities which are then activated through moral or spiritual exertion. Moreover, tying sanctification so firmly to divine agency enters a protest against exemplarist accounts of the atonement in which the work of Christ is reduced to the mere occasion, stimulus or pattern for the Christian's efforts to become holy through works of holiness.

Yet however decisive the backward reference of sanctification to justification, we may legitimately ask whether more needs to be maintained at this point if we are not to fall victim to a certain narrowness, a constriction of the scope of the Son's saving work. Two matters call for comment. First, without closer specification, insistence upon the centrality of justification for any account of sanctification may engender a certain abstraction of the work of the Son from his person, isolating the paschal events from the person and agent who is at their centre and, in effect, threatening to drift into a functionalist Christology in which the saviour's person is a mere function of his saving activity. This need not happen; indeed, any serious account of justification will want to resist rather strenuously any bifurcation of the Son's person and the Son's work. But that resistance will entail a reluctance to allow the motif of justification so to inflate itself that it bears the whole weight of the Son's work of reconciliation. Second, therefore, justification cannot be expected to function as a comprehensive summary for the reconciling work of the Son, but must be integrated into the wider sweep of the saving economy of God, which stretches from eternity to eternity, and whose centre is not justification alone, but the person and mission of the Son in its entirety – from his submission to the Father's will, through the assumption of flesh, the obedience and humiliation of incarnate existence, the proclamation and enactment of the kingdom of God, the giving of himself to death, the exaltation at resurrection and ascension to glory at the Father's right hand, and the continuing work as prophet, priest and king. It is that mission in its full compass, and not any single phase within it, which constitutes the achievement of our sanctification; only in that full compass do we have the enactment of the 'name' of Jesus Christ in which we are made holy.

What, then, does it mean that in this 'name' the Christian is sanctified? Simply this: Jesus Christ is the Holy One who makes holy. In the movement of his being as Son and Word made flesh, in his person and mission as 'the Holy One of God' (Mk 1.24), Jesus Christ sanctifies. By his existence and action, by the fact that he is the one whom the Father has consecrated (Jn 10.36), Jesus Christ makes holy. He does not only acquit, but, in acquitting, he consecrates, renewing humankind's vocation to be holy before God. He does not accomplish this in his person in isolation or in his work in isolation, for any such distinctions fail to catch the unitary identity of the person of the incarnate one. He sanctifies because as the one who assumes human nature he is in our place, and acts in our place, making us – not merely potentially, but actually – holy, consecrated to God. God made him our sanctification; to be a saint is to have one's holiness in Christ Jesus.

We ask again: 'Whence the miracle of human holiness?', and alongside our reference to the Father's work of election and the incarnate Son's work of reconciliation, we must return a third answer: we are sanctified 'in the Spirit of our God' (1 Cor. 6.11). The Holy Spirit is God himself active in 'realizing' or 'perfecting' the sanctification that is determined by the Father's creative will and established by the reconciling person and work of the Son. By the personal operation of the Spirit, that which God wills and accomplishes with sovereign freedom and effectiveness comes to be the actual condition of the Christian's existence: no longer an abstract state of affairs but an objective reality which gathers the Christian into itself. 'In' the Spirit, elected and accomplished sanctification is made effectual as the Christian's own most personal reality. God the Holy Spirit is, as Calvin puts it, 'the secret energy . . . by which we come to enjoy Christ and all his benefits'.[2]

This is – crucially – not to imprison the Spirit in the realm of human subjectivity. The secret energy of the sanctifying Spirit of God is not another way of talking of our own secret energies, and is not to be conceived as an infused power which stimulates human acts of holiness. To think in such terms would simply be to lose the reference of Christian holiness back to the triune work of grace, and turn sanctification into an acquired sufficiency. The Christian's sanctity is in Christ, in the Spirit, not *in se*; it is always and only an alien sanctity. Sanctification does not signal the birth of self-sufficiency, rather it indicates a 'perpetual and inherent lack of self-sufficiency'.[3] Sanctification 'in' the Spirit is not the Spirit's immanence in the saint. Quite the opposite: it is a matter of the *externality* of *sanctitas christiana*, the saint being and acting *in another*. 'Sanctification in the Spirit' means: it is not I who live, but Christ who lives in me. And 'Christ lives in me' means: by the Spirit's power I am separated from my self-caused self-destruction, and given a new holy self, enclosed by, and wholly referred to, the new Adam in whom I am and in whom I act.

III

All this is by way of stating that an account of the grounds of the holiness of the Christian requires a further extension of the language *sola gratia*, a reiteration of the *solus Deus* in the matter of the Christian life. How, consequently, is that life to be described? Our proposition continues thus: *Grounded in the electing, reconciling and perfecting work of Father, Son and Spirit,* the life for which the Christian is renewed is *the active life of holy fellowship* which *is the work of faith.*

Christian holiness is holy fellowship; it is the renewal of the relation to God which is the heart of holiness. To be a *creature* is to have one's being in relation to God, for 'to be' is 'to be in relation' to the creator, and only so to have life and to act. To be a *sinner* is to repudiate this relation, and so absolutely to imperil one's life by seeking to transcend creatureliness and become one's own origin and one's own end. This wicked refusal to be a creature cannot overturn the objectivity of the creator's determination to be God with us, for such is the creator's mercy that what he has resolved from all eternity stands fast. But the sinner's failure to live in acknowledgement of the creator's gift of life means that the creature chooses to torment and damage his being to the point of ruin, precisely by struggling out of the ordered relation to God in which alone the creature can be. To be a *reconciled sinner* is to be one in whom God's mercy has put an end to self-destruction, one whose enmity has been authoritatively and irrevocably overruled, and one therefore restored to life in relation to God. And, therefore, to be a *saint* is to be a reconciled sinner, re-established in fellowship and so liberated and empowered for the works of holiness.

In the divine work of sanctification, then, the creature is reintegrated into the movement of God's history with us, the history of active fellowship: though formerly the sinner struggled against that history and defied its Lord, now the sinner is consecrated to free and glad engagement with God. The older Protestant divines spoke of this in terms of the restoration of the image of God: the *terminus a quo* of sanctification is the corruption of the divine image, and sanctification's *terminus ad quem* is its restoration.[4] Language about the *imago Dei* can, of course, rather easily become excessively static, especially when the image is located in some human faculty such as reason or conscience, often with the purpose of furnishing a natural anthropological basis for talk of God. In view of this, it is perhaps wiser to conceive of the renewal of human nature 'after the image of its creator' (Col. 3.10) in terms which are as broad and as historical as possible: *anakainōsis* is the resumption of the history of fellowship between God and his creatures after the vile episode of sin; it is our comprehensive reintegration into the holy covenant by the mercy of the holy God.

On the side of the Christian, this fellowship which constitutes sanctification is the renewal of the active life of obedience. A passage near the beginning of Calvin's account of justification runs thus:

> Christ was given to us by God's generosity, to be grasped and possessed by faith. By partaking of him, we principally receive a double grace: namely, that being reconciled to God through Christ's blamelessness, we may have in heaven instead of a

Judge a gracious Father; and secondly, that sanctified by Christ's Spirit we may cultivate blamelessness and purity of life.[5]

In speaking of the reconciling work of God as a 'double grace', Calvin envisages the divine presence which encounters humankind in the gospel as the restoration of peace with God through divine acquittal, and as sanctification for active purity. Reconciled to God by God, we are made holy for the works of holiness.

This means that the works of holiness emerge from the convulsion and reorientation of human being and activity by God. In talking of what Calvin calls the 'cultivation' of blamelessness and purity of life, we do not fall back into self-realization: to that perversion of our creatureliness, God has uttered a final 'No' at the cross. Christian holiness is a matter of 'evangelical sanctification'[6] – of the holiness that the gospel *declares* and to which the creaturely counterpart is *faith*. Christian holiness is life in the space created by the presence of God's holiness through the reconciling Son and the consecrating Spirit. This is why 'we can . . . speak truly of sanctification *only* when we have understood the exceptionally great significance of the bond of *sola fide* and sanctification'.[7] Or, in Calvin's terms: sanctification is an aspect of the divine 'generosity', the grasping and possessing of which can only be 'in faith'.

The significance of *sola fide* in this context is, quite simply, immense. Not only does it underline the utter priority of grace, it also necessitates the development of a distinctive anthropology. For, if *sola fide* is the bass note of Christian holiness, then the explication of that holiness requires an ontology of the human person, and consequently a psychology and an ethics, in which the being of the Christian is not made but given. To be, and therefore to be holy, is to be an implicate of the creative and saving purposes of the triune God. Christian holiness is thus an aspect of the eschatological character of reconciled humanity. To be human in holy fellowship with God is to be granted one's being in the history of the triune God with us. In that history, the old, self-enclosed and polluted existence has been and is continually set aside, and a new existence opened up, a holy existence of fellowship with the Holy One. This new holy existence is 'eschatological' in that it emerges from the comprehensive overthrowing and reordering of human life and history which is called regeneration; and to that regenerative divine act there corresponds faith.

However, evangelical sanctification is not only the holiness that the gospel *declares* but also the holiness that the gospel *commands*, to which the creaturely counterpart is *action*. Holiness is indicative; but it is also imperative; indeed, it is imperative *because* it is the indicative holiness of the triune God whose work of sanctification is directed towards the renewal of the creature's active life of fellowship with him. Indicative holiness is no mere inert state in which we find ourselves placed and which requires nothing of us beyond passive acquiescence. Indicative holiness is the revelation of the inescapable conclusion under which our lives have been set – namely, that as those elected, justified and sanctified by the mercy of God, we are equally those who are determined for the active life of holiness. Because grace is 'double grace', it is election to activity. Double grace is always, of course, wholly *grace*; the active life of holiness is never apart from faith's assent to God's sheer creativity. But in a Christian theology of the holy life, grace is *duplex*, extending into the generation, evocation and preservation of action. 'Grace' – which is, of course, nothing other than a shorthand term for the great history of God's mercy, at whose centre is the passion and resurrection of Christ and his sending of the Spirit – is the gift of *life*, and life is active holiness in company with the holy God.

It is for this reason that it is very important not to isolate the motif of *sola fide* by making it into an absolute moment into which the entire moral psychology of the Christian collapses. The result of such isolation is always a drastic foreshortening of the life of Christian holiness, one which resists moralism by striking ethics from the gospel. This may be done under the banner of the doctrine of justification by grace through faith; but its result is a monism of justification that can scarcely hope to give an adequate account of the scope of the triune economy of grace. However indispensable *sola fide* may be, it should not be taken to mean that passivity is the only mode of Christian existence. *Sola fide* means that in all its acts, the being of the sanctified sinner refers to the lordly creativity of God – to the Father's electing mercy before all time, the Son's finished work, and the Spirit's presence and promise. Faith is ingredient within all holy activity; without faith such activity could not be holy. But faith has its setting in the entire economy of salvation, whose end is our renewal.

IV

This active life of holy fellowship is *at every moment character- ized by mortification and vivification.* As mortification, holiness is the laying aside of that which has been put to death at the cross of the Son of God; as vivification, holiness is the living out of that which has been made alive in the Son's resurrection. Mortification is thus a way of articulating how the new active life of the Christian succeeds and corresponds to the slaying of the old, death-laden existence of 'trespasses and sins'. Vivifica- tion speaks of the active life as corresponding to the great Easter reality: 'You he made alive!' (Eph. 2.1). Mortification and vivification, properly conceived, are not two separate acts, but the same reality differently viewed. Nor are mortification and vivification themselves distinct acts, distinguishable from other works of the Christian; rather, they are characteristics of all the patterns of activity that comprise the life of holiness. 'Putting to death' and 'putting on' are not acts alongside, or in addition to, other works; they are the character of the whole, seen in all its parts. Mortification and vivification signify the extension of the baptismal pattern into the life of the Christian, so that Christ's dying and rising, in – not despite – all their objectivity and perfection, are the shape of the Christian's own personal history. To live in the power and light of his death and resurrection, and under its tutelage, is to seek so to act that, in their own sphere and within their own very real limitations, our human lives give answer to grace.

The answer which is given is, depicted in the broadest terms, a laying aside of that which has already been abolished, and a living out of that which has no less definitively been established in the work of salvation. Of all the masters of the Reformation tradition, it is to Calvin that we must turn here once more, for he is the theologian of sanctification *par excellence*. In one of the many memorable passages in Book III of the *Institutes*, he writes:

> Now the great thing is this: we are consecrated and dedicated to God in order that we may thereafter think, speak, meditate, and do, nothing except to his glory. . .
>
> If we, then, are not our own but the Lord's, it is clear what error we must flee, and whither we must direct all the acts of our life. We are not our own: let not our reason nor our will, therefore, sway our plans and deeds. We are not our own: let us therefore not set it as our goal to seek what is expedient for us according to the flesh. We are not our own: in so far as we can, let us therefore forget ourselves and all that is ours.

Conversely, we are God's: let us therefore live for him and die for him. We are God's: let his wisdom and will therefore rule all our actions. We are God's: let all the parts of our life accordingly strive toward him as our only lawful goal. O, how much has that man profited who, having been taught that he is not his own, has taken away dominion and rule from his own reason that he may yield it to God! For, as consulting our self-interest is the pestilence that most effectively leads to our destruction, so the sole haven of salvation is to be wise in nothing and to will nothing through ourselves but to follow the leading of the Lord alone.[8]

What is the 'great thing' to which Calvin seeks to turn his readers' minds? The fact that our 'consecration' by God is *purposive* ('in order that . . .'); that we are sanctified *by* God *to* God; that the human end of the divine work of sanctification is that human reason, speech and action should be to the glory of God alone. From this there flows what Calvin sees as the twofold movement of the Christian life, a movement rooted in the twofold condition in which the Christian is placed. The condition is that, first, 'we are not our own', and, second, that we are 'the Lord's'. That is, negatively, in Christian existence we are irrevocably denied the right claimed by the sinner to self-possession and self-actualization, because, positively, we are possessed and made real by God. More briefly: our condition is one that denies our desire to be God to ourselves, because we have been created and recreated by the one true God. From this holy condition arises the movement of holy living, a movement which is at one and the same time an abandonment, a flight from falsehood and a turning – a directing of ourselves to the God in whom we *are*.

Mortification entails what Calvin goes on to describe as self-abandonment. 'Let this therefore be the first step, that a man depart from himself.'⁹ Of course, for Calvin this does not mean that the holy life spells the end of selfhood, but rather its extraction from the realm of wickedness, idolatry and rebellion. Reason and will are to be chastened, indeed mortified, not because their exercise is in and of itself depraved, but because they must be ordered away from self-chosen ends and so re-enter the service of God. This 'service', emptying human powers of their 'carnal' abuse, means 'obedience to God's Word' and a deference to the 'bidding of God's Spirit'.¹⁰ This is what Calvin, picking up an ancient theme, calls 'Christian philosophy' – wisdom for true human living in relation to God. It is chiefly known as giving place to God, submission and subjection which corresponds to the fact that the inflamed, proud, competent self, full of that jumble of desire and anxiety which is the sinner's grief, has been killed at the cross, and so can, and must, be abandoned.

Mortification, the older Protestant divines insisted, is not mere fleshly sorrow. It is quite other than the destructive misery we feel at the ruin which we have brought upon ourselves, which so quickly becomes self-hatred and hatred of God. Mortification is not despair in the face of the insolubility of our situation. Its dynamic is entirely different, for it is a turning away from that which has already been decisively dealt with by God in his reconciling work. Mortification is only possible because, at the cross, we 'have died', and because, by virtue of the resurrection, our life is 'hid with Christ in God' (Col. 3.3). Mortification is not hopeless self-accusation, but the setting aside of sin which can be undertaken and must be undertaken because sin has already been set aside. What characterizes mortification is thus not the frustrated rage of self-recrimination, but a horror at sin which flows from absolution, and a resolve to live out the release which God has won for us. Mortification, in other words, is inseparable from vivification, the *quickening* of life and activity which the gospel announces and to which we conform by directing 'all the acts of our life' towards the Lord.[11] *Sumus Domini* – We are the Lord's – is the great evangelical declaration that stands over the entirety of the life of Christian holiness. In it is set before us the fact that election has been fulfilled in reconciliation and perfected in the Spirit; by it, repentance is made possible as that truthful turn from the shadow of sin towards the light of life.

V

The active life of holy fellowship with God has mortification and vivification as its deep structure. That life is, finally, *actual as freedom, obedience and love.* The saint is one who is set free by God from sin and for reality; emancipated for obedience to the law which is God's moral truth for his creatures; and liberated for acts of love towards the neighbour in which human fellowship is preserved.

'Holiness' and 'freedom' are correlative terms: my sanctification is my emancipation. How is this so? Holiness is consecration by the work of the triune God in which I am set apart for service. By God's sanctifying grace I am rescued from the clutches of sin and death, and restored to life with the holy God. Holiness is restored covenant fellowship. That restored fellowship is, we must now see, both the root and the context of liberty. In fellowship with God, in the saints' communion with Father, Son and Spirit, we are given the strange gift of evangelical freedom. And in fellowship with God we are to exercise the freedom for which, according to the gospel, Christ has set us free.

But what is this strange gift of evangelical freedom? It is a *strange* gift because it can only be known and exercised as we are converted from a lie – the lie that liberty is unformed and

unconstrained self-actualization. It is *evangelical* because it is
grounded in the joyful reversal and reconstitution of the human
situation of which the gospel speaks. We may define it thus: In
evangelical freedom I am so bound to God's grace and God's call
that I am liberated from all other bonds and set free to live in the
truth. 'The law of the Spirit of life in Christ Jesus has set me free
from the law of sin and death' (Rom. 8.2). Freedom is inseparable from the law of the Spirit of life in Christ Jesus. That is, in
the mystery of the Son's achievement, present in the Spirit's
power, I am faced with a new, incontrovertible and omnipotent
reality – the reality of salvation which says that I am '*alive
because of righteousness*' (Rom. 8.10). This reality is 'law' in the
sense that it is a given truth which determines my present and
future and forms my action. But as such, it is also the ground of
my freedom, for in it is established the fact that I have been set
free from another law, 'the law of sin and death', emancipated
from self-destruction for life in reality.

Evangelical freedom cannot be divorced from the holy
fellowship with God of which it is an aspect. Fellowship with
God is both its basis and the sphere of its exercise. Drawn by the
divine mercy into holy fellowship, I am bound to God – I am,
in Paul's terms, a slave of Jesus Christ, my autonomy at last
broken. But bondage to Christ is not the antithesis of my freedom, quite the reverse: it is its essential condition. Why?
Because the Christ to whom I am bound is the one who has
finally secured the fact that no other power can come between
me and my flourishing. In him, God has set a *distance* between
me and all other bonds in which I find myself, and that distance
is 'the distance of freedom'.[12] Evangelical freedom is thus freedom from the powers that inhibit me (including, and especially,
my own powers). To live the active life of holy fellowship with
God is, therefore, to live out of the event of freedom from sin
and death. Evangelical freedom is the freedom that comes from

not being finally responsible for my own being; by the mercy of
God I am restored to know myself to be a creature in fellowship
with my creator and saviour. And to such freedom I cannot
liberate myself: self-liberation is precisely the 'yoke of slavery'
(Gal. 5.1) from which I have been set free.

Liberated and protected in this way, I am set free to live in
the truth. Modern accounts of freedom identify freedom as un-
fettered liberty for self-creation, and therefore contrast freedom
and nature: freedom is the antithesis of the given, a move
against and beyond any sense that I have a determinate identity.
Evangelical freedom, by contrast, does not envisage being
human as an utterly original making of life and history. Rather,
to be human is to live and act in conformity to the given truth
(nature) of what I am – a creature of grace, a reconciled sinner
and caught up in the movement of the ways and works of God
in which I am pointed to a perfection to be revealed in the last
times. I am free as I find myself finally unencumbered by idolatry, false desire and vanity, and therefore enabled to fill out,
actively to occupy and expand the role to which I am appointed.
In evangelical freedom I am set free for reality, and thus for the
practices of holiness. From this point of view, the polarization of
freedom and obedience that is endemic in modern anthropology is part of the pathology of the modern spiritual history of
the self. In the freedom given to me in Christ, I am bound to
God's grace. But God's grace is God's call; the holiness with
which God consecrates is also a command. And so freedom
involves conformity to the law. I am, in short, 'sanctified . . . for
obedience' (1 Pet. 1.2).

The form of the active life is law. Some Christian instincts
may initially prompt us to wariness at this point. We may fear
the use of the law as a means of acquiring righteousness, as it
were behind God's back, through 'works of the law'; or we may
associate the law with mere formality and externalism in morals

and religion that leaves the affections untouched. Law, certainly, may be an instrument of self-justification, or of decadent legalism. But properly – that is, evangelically – defined, law is the shape of the life which God commands of the elect. The degenerate use of the law can be countered only by integrating it into the covenant of grace which is the history of holiness. Abstracted from that covenant, law is certainly in league with sin and death; but within the drama of God's saving work, law is the given order of life, the trajectory along which our moral histories move. This is what is meant by the *usus didacticus* of the law: the law is a teacher, not a magistrate, instructing us in the way of holiness which flows from and corresponds to the goodness of God. Law rests on election and reconciliation; there is no retraction of grace here, and the recital of the law must always be prefaced by the words of God's liberating mercy: 'I am the Lord your God, who brought you out of the land of Egypt, out of the house of bondage' (Ex. 20.2). But the promise of grace engenders obedience. Holy obedience has two moments: teachableness and active service, a hearing and a doing of the will of God by which the reason, the affections and the will are all engaged in the service of the Holy One:

> Teach me, O Lord, the way of thy statutes;
> and I will keep it to the end.
> Give me understanding, that I may keep thy law
> and observe it with my whole heart.
> Lead me in the path of thy commandments,
> for I delight in it. (Ps. 119.33–35)

On the petition 'Give me understanding', Calvin comments thus:

> We are here informed that true wisdom consists in being wise according to the law of God, that it may preserve us in fear

and obedience to him. In asking God to confer this wisdom upon him, he owns that men, in consequence of their natural blindness, aim at anything rather than this. And, indeed, it is quite foreign to the notions usually prevalent among mankind to strain every nerve to keep God's law . . . For himself he asks no other prudence than the surrendering of himself entirely to God's direction.[13]

Freedom and obedience are thus both basic to the active life of holiness because they direct us outwards, away from sinful self-regard and towards life in the truth of God's law. It is for that reason that a portrait of the holy life can be completed by speaking of love alongside freedom and obedience. Liberated from wilful and fearful self-seeking, I am consecrated for works of love. Sanctification by God involves the restoration of society. For if evangelical freedom means my emancipation for the truth, and if evangelical obedience means my freedom to act within the righteous order of truth, then love is the free obedience in which I acknowledge my neighbour's cause and make it my own. Fellowship with God entails human fellowship. In the sphere of holiness, my neighbour is no longer a threat or an obstacle, nor a function of my self-interest. My neighbour is the presence to me of a truth which obliges me to act in his or her regard. Love, like freedom and obedience, involves mortification and vivification. Love is a counter-movement to our ruinous pride. '[T]here is no-one who does not cherish within himself some opinion of his own pre-eminence . . . each individual, by flattering himself, bears a kind of kingdom in his breast.'[14] That is why, Calvin continues, '[u]nless you give up all thought of self, and, so to speak, get out of yourself, you will accomplish nothing here'.[15] That giving up and getting out of self is mortification, and to it there corresponds the quickening of our regard for our fellows. Both dying to self and rising to love of neighbour are the fruits of the Spirit, perfecting in us the holiness for which we have been set apart by God.

Love involves my acknowledgement that I am *obliged* by my neighbour as a reality given to me by God, a reality which I would often like to evade but which encounters me with a transcendent imperative force. Why is this 'transcendent' ground for works of human fellowship theologically decisive? Because thereby my neighbour, the one with whom I stand in relation, is *given* to me, forming part of my destiny in the company of the saints. My neighbour is a summons to fellowship, because in him or her I find a claim on me that is not casual or fortuitous (and thereby dispensable) but rather precedes my will and requires that I act in my neighbour's regard. Without a sense that fellowship is (God-)given, my neighbour would not present a sufficiently strong claim to disturb me out of complacency and indifference into active, initiative-taking regard. Some basic acts of human fellowship – mercy to strangers, fidelity, patient attentiveness to the unlovely, devotion to long-standing and largely unreciprocated care of the comatose and handicapped – require for their sustenance a perception that the neighbour is one with whom I have been set in fellowship independent of (sometimes against) my will. My neighbour *obliges* me because he or she is the presence to me of the appointment and vocation of the holy God. Without givenness, without fellowship as more than a contingent fact, without the neighbour as a divine call, there is only my will. But, if fellowship is a condition and not merely one possibility for my ironic self to entertain, then in building common life – in culture, politics and ethics – I resist the relationlessness of sin into which I may drift, and, sanctified by Christ and Spirit, I realize my nature as one created for holiness.

We may draw these reflections to a close with a remembrance of the great seventeenth-century divine John Owen, who was Dean of Christ Church and Vice-Chancellor of Oxford under

Cromwell. Owen was not only the most considerable and prolific English Reformed theologian of his century, intellectually the equal of Hooker or Andrewes or any of the continental scholastic theologians of his period, but also a man of deep spiritual perception: a capacious and discriminating mind broken and remade by love of the gospel. Here, in closing, is what he had to say about what he called God's 'holy relations' to us – that is, of the holiness in which he turns to us:

> In thoughts of God, his saints rejoice at the remembrance of what he is, and what he will be unto them. Herein have they regard unto all the holy relations that he hath taken on himself towards them, with all the effects of his covenant in Christ Jesus . . . In these thoughts his saints take sweet delight; they are sweet unto them, and full of refreshment. Thus is it with those who are spiritually minded: they not only think much of God, but they take delight in these thoughts; they are sweet unto them; and not only so, but they have no solid joy nor delight, but in their thoughts of God, which therefore they retreat unto continually . . . [T]hose who are spiritually minded, will . . . continually betake themselves unto thoughts of God, wherein they find relief and refreshment against all that they feel and fear. In every state, their principal joy is in the remembrance of his holiness.[16]

And so: as Father, God is the one who wills and purposes from all eternity the separation of humankind as a holy people, destined for fellowship with himself. As Son, God is the one who achieves this separation of humankind by rescuing humanity from its pollution and bondage to unholiness. As Spirit, God is the one who completes or perfects that separation by sanctifying humankind and drawing it into righteous fellowship with the holy God. May it be so with us.

Conclusion

In the preceding chapters, I have tried to articulate and defend two basic proposals, one about the way in which Christian theology goes about the task of giving an account of holiness, and another about the material content of such an account. The first proposal was that a dogmatics of holiness is itself an exercise of holiness. Christian theological thinking, if it is to take place in the midst of the common life of the saints of God, is not transcendent critical inquiry but an attempt at rational speech about the Holy One. A Christian theology of holiness is an exercise of holy reason, and holy reason is reason segregated by God so that God's communicative presence as Father, Son and Spirit can be known and loved. Both the context and the content of what Christian theology has to say about holiness derive from revelation (the gift of God's presence as the Holy One); and so such a theology is not poetic but positive, not an activity of naming but one of confessing. It finds its content, its norm and its limit in Holy Scripture as the inspired creaturely instrument through which the Holy One announces himself. Accordingly, its primary task is exegetical rather than comparative or phenomenological. It tries as best it can to read the canon as a witness to God's self-promulgation, and is unpersuaded that much is to be gained from reading the canon as an expression of the experience of the holy-in-general. Such an account, I suggest, cannot be the work of unaided reason, for reason, too, is caught up in the history of holiness; reason is part of the history of wickedness and the overcoming of wickedness by the reconciling and sanctifying works of God. Thus as 'holy reason', Christian theology will properly display the traces of mortification and vivification, as it is reproved for its vanity and love of falsehood and remade by the Spirit for humble attention to truth. Its fundamental posture will thus be prayerful; and its place will be in the fellowship of the saints, serving the community's confession of the triune God, the fearing and sanctifying of God's name.

The second proposal made in the course of the preceding discussions concerned the content of a Christian theology of holiness. That content was set out by exploring three inseparable themes: the holiness which is proper to the Holy Trinity; the holiness of the Church; and the holiness of the individual Christian. The inseparability of these themes derives from the inner structure of Christian beliefs about God's trinitarian holiness. As Father, Son and Spirit, God's holiness is a way of indicating the 'name' and 'works' of God, that is, the identity which God enacts. Like all talk of God's attributes, talk of God's holiness is a conceptual attempt to point to the concreteness of God's identity. That concrete identity is 'enacted' in the sense that it is accomplished in God's free action towards his creatures as creator, reconciler and perfecter. Holiness is thus God's personal moral relation to his creatures. The triune Holy One is the one who establishes fellowship: as Father willing and forming the creature for fellowship, as Son defending that fellowship against the offensive of sin, and as Spirit bringing that fellowship to its human completion. Holiness as a mode of relation can be explored at two levels; the ecclesial and the individual. Ecclesial holiness is grounded in the work of the Holy Trinity in electing, redeeming and consummating a holy people who are the covenant partners of God and the fellowship of the saints. The

Church's holiness is thus always an alien sanctity: gift, not possession; grace, not achievement. It is, moreover, visible in the primary act of the Church, which is confession – that is, acknowledgement or recognition of the sheer majesty, transcendent worth and goodness of God. Holiness is not self-achieved perfection but a pointing to the perfect reality of the holy God. Its primary forms are hearing the command and promise of the gospel, confession of sin in penitence and faith, testimony before the world, and prayer for the hallowing of God's name. At the level of individual sanctification, holiness is the creature's renewal by the work of the Holy Trinity, in which the creature is emancipated for the active life of fellowship with God. Through sanctification, the creature is reintegrated into the movement of God's history with us. All holy activity flows from faith; but faith is active in the baptismal pattern of dying and rising with Christ, that is, in mortification and vivification, through which holiness is shaped as freedom, obedience and love.

Such thoughts, lovely though they would have been for many in the Christian past, are scarcely conceivable in our culture. Unlike, for example, tolerance, holiness is not esteemed a civic virtue, and strikes us as inhumane. That is not because it is inhumane; quite the opposite: for the Christian confession, holiness is ingredient within human flourishing. If the opposite seems to be the case, it is in part because understanding holiness and engaging in its practices require the conversion of our conception of humanity. What might be involved in that conversion?

We are schooled by our culture to organize our sense of our own identities in a *reflexive* way. That is to say, we are less likely to receive our primary self-understanding from given localities, traditions and roles, and more likely to act in ways whose manner and goal is self-construction. Lacking by and large any deep vocabulary of natures and ends in both our politics and our moral psychology, we gravitate by instinct towards voluntarism, though it is a voluntarism of a particular variety. It is (at least in the high modern West) not so much a voluntarism of rebellion, but rather one of consumption and style. In the Kantian and Marxist forms which exercised such a powerful force in the nineteenth and twentieth centuries, the voluntarism of rebellion retained a sense that to be human was to be a certain kind of being, one with a specific destiny – the project of liberation. The voluntarism of consumption and style differs from this in two crucial respects. It lacks that sense of the identity and durability of the human which is articulated in talk of human 'nature', preferring a much more differential or revisable account of what it means to be human. And it is largely non-teleological; such ends as we may set for ourselves are local, transient, and not a movement towards the perfection of our natures, for we have none to perfect. Consider, for example, the following passage from the second volume of Foucault's *History of Sexuality*:

[F]or an action to be 'moral,' it must not be reducible to an act or series of acts conforming to a rule, a law, or a value. Of course all moral action involves a relationship with the reality in which it is carried out, and a relationship with the self. The latter is not simply 'self-awareness' but self-formation as an 'ethical subject', a process in which the individual delimits what part of himself will form the object of his moral practice, defines his position relative to the precept he will follow, and decides on a certain mode of being that will serve as his moral goal. And this requires him to act upon himself, to monitor, test, improve, and transform himself. There is no specific moral action that does not refer to a unified moral conduct; no moral conduct that does not call for the forming of oneself as an ethical subject; and no forming of the ethical subject without 'modes of subjectivation' and an 'ascetics' or 'practices of the self' that support them.[1]

Foucault's concern here is not simply the characteristically modern worry that conformity to external norms does not secure moral authenticity. It is much more that being an ethical subject is a matter of self-formation. Morality is a practice of the self, 'what might be called "the determination of ethical substance"; that is, the way in which the individual has to constitute this or that part of himself as the prime material of his moral conduct'.[2] It is that '*ethical work* that one performs on oneself . . . to attempt to transform oneself into the ethical subject of one's behaviour'.[3] This collapse of morality into self-stylization (what Foucault calls 'ascetics') not only entails the most severe contraction of moral ontology; it also makes acutely difficult any conception of moral obligation, for behind style lies *will*, unattached, and, without ends, unchastened.

Again, consider Anthony Giddens' definition of 'life politics' in *Modernity and Self-Identity*:

Life politics presumes (a certain level of) emancipation . . . : emancipation from the fixities of tradition and from the conditions of hierarchical domination . . . Life politics does not primarily concern the conditions which liberate us in order to make choices: it is a politics *of* choice. While emancipatory politics is a politics of life chances, life politics is a politics of lifestyle. Life politics is the politics of a reflexively mobilised order – the system of late modernity – which, on an individual and collective level, has radically altered the parameters of social activity. It is a politics of self-actualisation in a reflexively ordered environment, where that reflexivity links self and body to systems of global scope. In this arena of

activity, power is generative rather than hierarchical. Life
politics is lifestyle politics in the serious and rich sense.[4]

Giddens' language is less drastically internal, more public, than
that of Foucault; but the underlying vision of selfhood organized around choice, the centrality of style, and the inconse-
quential status of nature as a domain external to the self's
manipulation, remain much the same. There is no nature and
no historical course other than those cast up in the processes of
'the reflexive project of the self'.[5]

With such construals of human identity, a Christian theology
of holiness is simply incommensurable. According to the
Christian confession, the space in which human living is undertaken is created and reconciled space which is on the way to
its final perfection. Created and recreated by God and ordered
by God's providential presence, it is a given space with a given
historical trajectory. In that spatial and temporal domain,
human work is the work of beings whose self-definition is not
their own project but a responsible endeavour truthfully and
faithfully to live out the calling of the Holy One. Responsibility
does not mean the end of all human mobility or plasticity, for
it is characteristic of the kind of creature that we are that we
discover our identity by fulfilling a vocation through time; we
become holy. But the becoming is, precisely, discovery, not
invention; it is not our generation of a self-narrative, not life
politics or an ascetics (aesthetics) of the self, but the enactment
of an office: 'You shall be holy, for I, the Lord your God, am
holy.'

Such affirmations about human life in the domain and
history of holiness appear deeply traditionalist and therefore
essentialist, as indeed in certain respects they are; a culture
which aspires to be detraditionalized and to repudiate essences
may have little taste for them. But it should not be overlooked

that the history of holiness is not simply regular, consistent and steady; it is an eschatological history, generated by baptism, and its ontology is organized around the advent of newness. It is the baptized, not the devotees of 'secular risk culture',[6] who ought to be familiar with their own dissolution, and therefore with their remaking.

Persuading our culture that holiness is of paramount importance for its well-being will require not only the culture's conversion, but also the continual conversion of the Church to the gospel of holiness. A crucial aspect of holiness is an increase in *concentration*: the focusing of mind, will and affections on the holy God and his ways with us. This book has been an attempt at such concentration. Promoting concentration is not the work of theology, however, but of God, and so it is a matter for prayer. At the end of one of the lectures which Calvin gave on Ezekiel in 1563–4, the last lectures he was to give, he prayed thus:

> Almighty God, in your limitless goodness you have deemed us worthy of such an honour that you descended to earth in the person of your only-begotten Son, and each day appear to us intimately in your gospel where we contemplate your living image. Therefore grant that we may not abuse such a benefit through senseless curiosity but be truly transformed into your glory, and thus more and more advance in the renewal of our minds and entire life, so that at last we may be gathered into that blessed and eternal glory which has been obtained for us through your only-begotten Son, our Lord. Amen.[7]

Notes

Introduction

1. K. Barth, *Protestant Theology in the Nineteenth Century: Its Background and History*, London: SCM Press, 2001, pp. 444–5.

Chapter 1

1. K. Barth, 'Revelation', in *God in Action*, Edinburgh: T&T Clark, 1936, p. 17.

2. E. Farley, *Divine Empathy: A Theology of God*, Minneapolis: Fortress Press, 1996, p. 79.

3. See R. Otto, *The Idea of the Holy*, Oxford: Oxford University Press, 1923, pp. 12–24.

4. P. Tillich, *Systematic Theology*, vol. 1, Chicago: University of Chicago Press, 1951, p. 215.

5. J. Derrida, 'Faith and Knowledge: the Two Sources of "Religion"', in J. Derrida and G. Vattimo, (eds), *Religion*, Cambridge: Polity Press, 1998, p. 36.

6. J. Calvin, *The Epistles of Paul the Apostle to the Romans and to the Thessalonians*, Edinburgh: St Andrew Press, 1961, pp. 32–3.

7. H. Cremer, *Die christliche Lehre von den Eigenschaften Gottes*, Giessen: Brunnen-Verlag, 1983, p. 43.

8. K. Barth, *Evangelical Theology: An Introduction*, New York: Holt, Rinehart & Winston, 1963, p. 160.

9. Barth, *Evangelical Theology*, p. 37.

10. G. Aulén, *The Faith of the Christian Church*, London: SCM Press, 1954, p. 123.

11. J. Edwards, *Dissertation I. Concerning the End for Which God Created the World*, in *Works, 8: Ethical Writings*, New Haven: Yale University Press, 1989, p. 442.

Chapter 2

1. Cf. J. Calvin, *Institues of the Christian Religion*, I.x.2, ET John T. McNeill (ed.) and F. L. Battles (trans.), Library of Christian Classics XX, Philadelphia: Westminster Press, 1960, pp. 97–8.

2. Calvin, *Institutes* I.x.1 (ET p. 97).

3. P. Tillich, *Systematic Theology*, vol. 1, Chicago: University of Chicago Press, 1951, p. 215.

4. In his treatment of the divine attributes in *The God of the Philosophers*, Oxford: Clarendon Press, 1979, Anthony Kenny, for example, focuses on omnipresence and omnipotence; 'other attributes, such as justice, mercy, and love, have a more obvious significance for the religious believer; but they are also less immediately amenable to philosophical investigation and analysis' (p. 5); note the restrictiveness of an analytical method which is incapable of making much philosophical sense of positive religious belief and practice, and which therefore has to limit itself to the investigation of belief in a god by no one in particular. R. Swinburne, similarly, elides the force of the notion of holiness as he reduces the divine attributes to their simplest possible form, in which all the divine properties 'follow from a very simple property which I shall call having pure, limitless, intentional power': *The Christian God*, Oxford: Clarendon Press, 1994, p. 151; the effect of this formal definition is to factor out the difference which would be made by a material or directional determination of the divine being out of the divine activity. Other accounts of the divine attributes which offer no treatment of holiness include: R. M. Gale, *On the Nature and Existence of God*, Cambridge: Cambridge University Press, 1991; E. R. Wierenga, *The Nature of God: An Inquiry into Divine Attributes*, Ithaca, NY: Cornell University Press, 1989; J. Hoffman and G. Rosenkrantz, (eds), *The Divine Attributes*, Oxford: Blackwell, 2002.

5. On the significance of the relation of God's essence to God's existence for a material definition of God, see E. Jüngel, *God as the Mystery of the World*, Grand Rapids: Eerdmans, 1983, pp. 100–9.

6. See here M. Buckley, *At the Origins of Modern Atheism*, New Haven: Yale University Press, 1987.

7. C. Schwöbel, *God, Action and Revelation*, Kampen: Kok Pharos, 1992, p. 47; cf. C. Gunton, *The Christian Faith*, Oxford: Blackwell, 2002, pp. 188–91.

8. Schwöbel, *God, Action and Revelation*, p. 50.

9. *Contra* W. Pannenberg's argument that the predicative use of the word 'God' is prior to and underlies its nominal use (*Systematic Theology*, vol. 1, Grand Rapids: Eerdmans, 1991, pp. 67–8, 70 n. 21).

10. Augustine, *De Trinitate*, VI.iv.6 (my translation).

11. Augustine, *De Trinitate*, VI.iv.6.

12. H. Heppe, *Reformed Dogmatics*, London: Allen & Unwin, 1950, p. 59.

13. C. Hodge has an acute treatment of the dangers of denying any real distinctions between the divine attributes in *Systematic Theology*, London: Nelson, 1877, vol. 1, pp. 371–4.

14. P. Mastricht, cited in Heppe, *Reformed Dogmatics*, p. 60.

15. E. Jüngel, 'Theses on the Relation of the Existence, Essence and Attributes of God', *Toronto Journal of Theology* 17 (2001), p. 66.

16. Jüngel, 'Theses', p. 66.

17. D. Staniloae, *Orthodox Dogmatic Theology: The Experience of God*, Brookline: Holy Cross Orthodox Press, 1994, p. 223.

18. Cf. G. von Rad, *Old Testament Theology*, vol. 1, Edinburgh: Oliver & Boyd, 1962, p. 206, on the way in which in Israel holiness is 'much more rigorously bound to Jahweh himself'.

19. T. Tracy, *God, Action, and Embodiment*, Grand Rapids: Eerdmans, 1984, p. 19.

20. Tracy, *God, Action, and Embodiment*, p. 20; cf. Schwöbel, *God, Action, and Revelation*, pp. 58–9.

21. Jüngel, 'Theses', 3.7.1, 3.7.2, 5.5.1; cf. W. Krötke, *Gottes Klarheiten. Eine Neuinterpretation der Lehre von Gottes 'Eigenschaften'*, Tübingen: Mohr, 2001, who suggests that 'every attribute of God must be unfolded on the basis of God's movement towards the world, as it was an event in the history of Jesus Christ and remains an event in the Holy Spirit' (p. 114).

22. von Rad, *Old Testament Theology*, vol. 1, p. 205.

23. H. Bavinck, *The Doctrine of God*, Edinburgh: Banner of Truth Trust, 1991, p. 213.

24. From this point of view, questions might be raised about the distinction drawn by Staniloae between holiness as a quality of the Holy Trinity, which is 'apophatic and undefinable' and therefore properly called 'supra-holiness' (Staniloae, *Orthodox Dogmatic Theology*, p. 222), and holiness as a divine relation to creatures. Even though Staniloae does go on to concede that '[i]n the holiness manifested in the world the same combination of the transcendent and the revealed, of elevation and condescension in God is revealed' (p. 222), the

difficulty of counter-poising majesty and relation remains unresolved. Similarly, Tillich suggests that holiness as relation is 'paradoxical':

> The unapproachable character of God, or the impossibility of having a relation with him in the proper sense of the word, is expressed in the word 'holiness'. God is essentially holy, and every relation to him involves the consciousness that it is paradoxical to be related to that which is holy. God cannot become an object of knowledge or a partner in action. If we speak, as we must, of the ego-thou relation between God and man, the thou embraces the ego and consequently the entire relation . . . Ultimately, it is an insult to the divine holiness to talk about God as we do of objects whose existence or non-existence can be discussed. It is an insult to the divine holiness to treat God as a partner with whom one collaborates or as a superior power whom one influences by rites and prayers. The holiness of God makes it impossible to draw him into the context of the ego-world and the subject-object correlation. He himself is the ground and meaning of this correlation, not an element within it. (Tillich, *Systematic Theology*, vol. 1, pp. 271–2)

But because it is not undergirded by a trinitarian account of the relation of God and creatures, Tillich's account tends to polarize intrinsic and extrinsic holiness; without an account of the free relatedness of the triune God, its only safeguard against immanentizing divine holiness is the dogmatically bare notion of 'paradox'. Brunner speaks in similarly abstract terms of 'the dialectic of Holiness and Love' (E. Brunner, *The Christian Doctrine of God: Dogmatics*, vol. 1, London: Lutterworth Press, 1949, p. 163).

25. This relation cannot be stated through the categories of a non-personal metaphysics, but requires that the language of personal agency and historical relation be left to stand as irreducible. Izaak Dorner in his (otherwise admirable) treatment of divine holiness in the Old Testament notes that holiness is 'no mere negative or transcendent attribute of God, but is also of positive value in the realization of the world' (I. Dorner, *System of Christian Doctrine*, Edinburgh: T&T Clark, 1880, vol. 1, p. 322); but he goes on (p. 323) to state this communication of holiness in non-personal terms: 'It creates a new spiritual life by applying its soul, Holiness, to the propagation of itself in the world' – note how the immediate effect of translating out of the category of personal relation is to elide the distinction (and therefore,

of course, the relation) of God and the world. Pannenberg, similarly, adopts a Hegelian framework for articulating divine holiness, suggesting a 'structural affinity between what the Bible says about the holiness of God and the concept of the true Infinite. The Infinite that is merely a negation of the finite is not yet truly seen as the Infinite (as Hegel showed), for it is defined by delimitation from something else, i.e., the finite . . . The Infinite is truly infinite only when it transcends its own antithesis to the finite. In this sense the holiness of God is truly infinite, for it is opposed to the profane, yet it also enters the profane world, penetrates it, and makes it holy' (W. Pannenberg, *Systematic Theology*, vol. 1, p. 400). The absence of language of holiness as willed relation is striking here; Pannenberg's talk of 'the essence of God as Spirit' which expresses 'the fact that the transcendent God himself is characterized by a vital movement which causes him to invade what is different from himself and to give it a share in his own life' (p. 400) moves in a rather different direction.

26. H. Martensen, *Christian Dogmatics*, Edinburgh: T&T Clark, 1898, p. 92.

27. G. Aulén, *The Faith of the Christian Church*, London: SCM Press, 1954, p. 121.

28. See, for example, E. Schlink, *Ökumenische Dogmatik. Grundzüge*, Göttingen: Vandenhoeck & Ruprecht, 1983, pp. 760–1; Krötke, *Gottes Klarheiten*, p. 116.

29. Cremer, *Die christliche Lehre von den Eigenschaften Gottes*, p. 45.

30. F. D. E. Schleiermacher, *The Christian Faith*, ET Edinburgh: T&T Clark, 1928, p. 194. See E. Farley, *Divine Empathy*, for a sophisticated contemporary equivalent. I am unconvinced by G. Ebeling's attempt to read Schleiermacher as 'relational', not 'subjective': see 'Schleiermachers Lehre von den göttlichen Eigenschaften', in *Wort und Glaube* II, Tübingen: Mohr, 1969, pp. 305–42.

31. Schleiermacher, *The Christian Faith*, p. 195.

32. Schlink, *Ökumenische Dogmatik*, p. 761.

33. I. Kant, *Lectures on the Philosophical Doctrine of Religion*, in A. W. Wood and G. di Giovanni, (eds), *Religion and Rational Theology*, Cambridge: Cambridge University Press, 1996, p. 409.

34. Mastricht, cited in Heppe, *Reformed Dogmatics*, p. 93.

35. Cremer, *Die christliche Lehre von den Eigenschaften Gottes*, p. 36.

36. Brunner, *The Christian Doctrine of God: Dogmatics* vol. 1, p. 160.

37. Gunton, *The Christian Faith*, p. 49. It is a fundamental weakness of J. Armstrong's argument in *The Idea of Holiness and the Humane*

Response, London: Allen & Unwin, 1981, that it fails to discern the tie between holiness and maintenance of the creature's cause; this failure leads to the claim that in the biblical tradition we find 'holiness as absolute centralised power' (p. 15) – what Armstrong terms 'sacralism' –and that 'fully developed holiness licenses, nay demands, holy genocide' (p. 94). There is a serious question underlying the book's exegetical and historical absurdities, but its tendentiousness simply obscures its force.

38. J. Edwards, *Dissertation I. Concerning the End for Which God Created the World*, in *Works, 8: Ethical Writings*, New Haven: Yale University Press, 1989, p. 433.

Chapter 3

1. K. Barth, *Church Dogmatics*, IV/1, Edinburgh: T&T Clark, 1956, p. 693. Cf. H. Küng, *The Church*, London: Search Press, 1968, pp. 325–6.

2. I am much less disposed to see ecclesial identity as the core theme of Ephesians, and much more disposed to find an underlying theology of grace, than is D. Ford in his account of the letter in *Self and Salvation: Being Transformed*, Cambridge: Cambridge University Press, 1999, pp. 107–36.

3. See Col. 3.12 and 1 Pet. 1.2.

4. J. Calvin, *The Epistles of Paul the Apostle to the Galatians, Ephesians, Philippians and Colossians*, Edinburgh: Oliver & Boyd, 1965, pp. 124–5.

5. Calvin, *Galatians, Ephesians, Philippians and Colossians*, p. 125.

6. Calvin, *Galatians, Ephesians, Philippians and Colossians*, p. 125

7. See, for just one example, W. Meeks, *The First Urban Christians: The Social World of the Apostle Paul*, New Haven: Yale University Press, 1983, pp. 74–110, in which the eschatological character of election to holiness is thoroughly immanentized.

8. Calvin, *Galatians, Ephesians, Philippians and Colossians*, p. 207.

9. Calvin, *Galatians, Ephesians, Philippians and Colossians*, p. 156.

10. Barth, *Church Dogmatics*, IV/1, p. 654.

11. M. Luther, *Werke. Weimarer Ausgabe* 34/I, 276.7f.; cf. E. Jüngel, 'The Church as Sacrament?', in *Theological Essays I*, Edinburgh: T&T Clark, 1999, p. 210, who comments that 'Luther found in the Church's recognition of its own sinfulness a proof of its true holiness.'

12. K. Barth, *The Christian Life*, Grand Rapids: Eerdmans, 1981, pp. 115–16.

13. Barth, *The Christian Life*, p. 163.

14. Barth, *The Christian Life*, p. 163.

15. Barth, *The Christian Life*, p. 157.

16. Barth, *The Christian Life*, p. 169.

Chapter 4

1. J. Edwards, *Charity and Its Fruits*, in *Works, 8: Ethical Writings*, New Haven: Yale University Press, 1989, pp. 294–5.

2. J. Calvin, *Institutes of the Christian Religion*, III.i.1, ET John T. McNeill (ed.) and F. L. Battles (trans.), Library of Christian Classics XX, Philadelphia: Westminster Press, 1960, p. 537.

3. G. C. Berkouwer, *Faith and Sanctification*, Grand Rapids: Eerdmans, 1952, p. 83.

4. See H. Heppe, *Reformed Dogmatics*, London, Allen & Unwin, 1950, p. 565.

5. Calvin, *Institutes*, III.xi.1 (ET p. 725).

6. H. Bavinck, *Gereformeerde Dogmatiek*, Kampen: Kok, 1928, vol. 4, p. 233.

7. Berkouwer, *Faith and Sanctification*, p. 42

8. Calvin, *Institutes*, III.vii.1 (ET p. 690).

9. Calvin, *Institutes*, III.vii.1 (ET p. 690).

10. Calvin, *Institutes*, III.vii.1 (ET p. 690).

11. Calvin, *Institutes*, III.vii.1 (ET p. 690).

12. H. Berkhof, *Christian Faith*, Grand Rapids: Eerdmans, 1986, p. 459.

13. J. Calvin, *Commentary on the Book of Psalms*, Edinburgh: Calvin Translation Society, 1847, vol. 4, p. 425.

14. Calvin, *Institutes*, III.vii.4 (ET p. 694).

15. Calvin, *Institutes*, III.vii.5 (ET p. 695).

16. J. Owen, ΦΡΟΝΗΜΑ ΤΟΥ ΠΝΕΥΜΑΤΟΣ *or the grace and duty of being spiritually minded declared and practically improved*, in *Works*, Edinburgh: Banner of Truth Trust, 1965, vol. 7, pp. 364–5.

Conclusion

1. M. Foucault, *The Uses of Pleasure: The History of Sexuality, Volume 2*, London: Penguin, 1992, p. 28.

2. Foucault, *The Uses of Pleasure*, p. 26.

3. Foucault, *The Uses of Pleasure*, p. 27.

4. A. Giddens, *Modernity and Self-Identity: Self and Society in the Late Modern Age*, Stanford: Stanford University Press, 1991, p. 214; cf. A. Giddens, *The Consequences of Modernity*, Cambridge: Polity Press, 1990.

5. Giddens, *Modernity and Self-Identity*, p. 231.

6. Giddens, *Modernity and Self-Identity*, p. 181.

7. J. Calvin, *Ezekiel I (Chapters 1–12)*, Grand Rapids: Eerdmans, 1994, p. 57.

Index